JOSEPHINE BUTLER

May,

Josephine is quite a
woman!

as ever. *[signature]*

JOSEPHINE BUTLER

A Guide to her Life, Faith and Social Action

Rod Garner

DARTON · LONGMAN + TODD

First published in 2009 by
Darton, Longman and Todd Ltd
1 Spencer Court
140 – 142 Wandsworth High Street
London
SW18 4JJ

ISBN 978-0-232-52747-6

A catalogue record for this book is available from the British Library

Phototypeset by YHT Ltd, London
Printed and bound in Great Britain by
Athenaeum Press, Gateshead, Tyne & Wear

Contents

Introduction

✦┼┤══════┼┼══════├┼✦

I REMEMBER 4 JULY 2008 very well. My wife
Christine and I were preparing to make a long journey
home after a short break in the Highlands. A week of
indifferent weather had finally given way to a perfect day
of warm, bright sunshine and the gentlest of breezes.
Before setting off, we had decided to make a significant
detour that would take us through many miles of restful
Northumberland countryside. Our aim was to visit the
little parish church of St Gregory the Great in Kirknewton. Not quite a pilgrimage to a holy place in the accepted
sense, but rather a mutual need to pay our respects at the
grave of the remarkable woman whose final resting-place
can be found in the churchyard just to the west of the
church tower.

St Gregory's stood unobtrusively off a quiet road. Apart
from the noise of a few passing vehicles, there was a
perceptible calm. Enchantment best describes our reaction
to the stillness and beauty we found all around us. We
located the grave, read the simple inscription and stood for
several minutes before entering the church. In the porch
we saw a sculpture and a stained-glass window commis-
sioned by the PCC to mark the centenary of the death of
Josephine Butler in 2006. The bars and bindweed at the
base of the sculpture symbolise oppression and pain. These
transform into lilies which are a traditional symbol of the
resurrection of Christ. They represent the testimony of a
woman who brought courage and an indomitable will to a

long struggle on behalf of 'the poor, the weak and friendless'. She believed that a God of hope and justice was on their side and that they should not be left to perish as outcasts in a society that had held them to be of little or no account. She did all this in an attitude of prayer and waiting that sometimes brought her anguish and pain. But she also radiated beauty, intelligence, warmth and compassion along with a gift of speaking that could electrify the hearts and minds of ordinary working men and women and confront those in positions of power. She was a Christian with a deep love of Christ but no great enthusiasm for organised religion. She was a woman finely attuned to the needs and challenges of changing times and the deviousness of the human heart when vested interests are challenged. Her achievements brought to an end a long night of Victorian hypocrisy, cruelty and violence towards women. Many came to know her personally and were transformed by the encounter.

I made the pilgrimage to Northumberland and I have written this short book for particular reasons. A generation ago Josephine Butler was in danger of becoming a forgotten saint. Thankfully, she is now being rediscovered. My own Anglican cathedral in Liverpool has a stained-glass window in her honour and she is remembered in the Church of England's calendar on the day of her baptism, 30 May. Books are once again being written about her and she has become the subject of serious academic discussion as a woman and 'a proto feminist' so obviously 'ahead of her age'. My own concern is that she should become more widely known not just as a social reformer but also as a singular and special human being with an extraordinary capacity for living and endurance. She is able to speak to the confusion and darkness of our own fragmented age and offers us a beauty that softens and inspires. She is not without flaws, and this too is part of her attraction!

The invitation to extend the literature on Josephine came as a result of a gathering of academics and clergy that I attended in the Autumn of 2006. Over four days we presented papers reflecting different aspects of her life and work, and these duly appeared in book form the following Summer.[1] Before leaving the assembly, I was asked over lunch if I would consider writing a study guide that would be helpful to individuals and groups ready to learn more about this eminent Victorian. Despite a deadline to complete another book that I was already working on, I felt it was right to accept the commission. During the past ten years Josephine has become a gentle but pervasive influence in my life. In the best possible way, she has got under my skin, and my admiration and respect for her continue to grow.

Treasure of any kind exists to be shared, and my hope is that by reading these pages you will feel a similar indebtedness and a strengthening of your own faith. They need to be read thoughtfully and prayerfully, and I have provided additional material at the end of each chapter for this purpose. Josephine raises many important questions and you will find her a stimulating conversation partner.

In what follows you can trace her life story, her approach to marriage, prayer and politics, and her social witness in the service of compassion, justice and truth. You will also find in the occasional asides, touching glimpses of a loving partnership of true equals and a vulnerable yet brave woman whose reputation as one of the outstanding figures of the nineteenth century is entirely deserved.

I gladly acknowledge here the work of others that has

assisted and stimulated my own portrait. In particular, the splendid biography written by Jane Jordan.[2] I have returned to it many times in recent years and rarely without profit or pleasure. My thanks as always go to my wife Christine and our sons Daniel and George, who were enthusiastic when the writing seemed to flow and supportive when it faltered! Special thanks also to my former parish administrator Ruby Smith. This is the fifth book she has processed, proof-read or indexed for me in as many years. She has done all this without ever once saying 'enough is enough' or losing the will to live! She has proved a trusted work partner and the embodiment of Christian patience. I remain deeply grateful to her.

Chapter 1

EMINENT VICTORIAN:
AHEAD OF HER AGE

T HE YEAR 1828 HAD its modest share of historic
events. The Duke of Wellington became Prime
Minister. London Zoo was opened and John Payne Collier
produced a script of *Punch and Judy* to make hard times
more tolerable for the masses. In the world of crime and
punishment, Sir Robert Peel's innovatory police force
came into being with just 101 uniformed officers and 5
civil servants. Less than three months later and with a
conspicuous lack of Christmas cheer, the trial began on 17
December of the notorious murderers and body-snatchers
Burke and Hare.

Also in that year, Josephine Elizabeth Grey was born on
13 April in Glendale, Northumberland. She was the seventh
of ten children born to Hannah and John Grey. From them
she imbibed her religion and her moral point of view and to
them she owed the cultivation of her creative gifts. Josephine excelled at the piano, and to the end of her long life,
she treasured the two bound volumes of Beethoven sonatas
given to her by her mother. Hannah also supervised her
education, encouraged her to paint and remained a
dependable parent to whom Josephine could always turn.

John was a much-loved father, at ease with his children, a gentle giant who encouraged his daughters to dance and play and amused them on repeated occasions by his inability to knot his neck-tie – 'a mystery he could never compass', as Josephine noted in a later memoir. If his lack of sartorial skills made for mirth in the household, his moral force as a landowner, a Justice of the Peace and a member of the national movement to abolish slavery, helped to shape Josephine's passion against injustice. She revered and remembered her father as a champion of great causes, a lover of liberty and a Christian of wide sympathies. As a landlord he lived the gospel principles he taught, improving tenants' conditions and wages and providing education for every child. Often his voice would tremble when he spoke to his children about slavery and the stain it constituted on his country's character. He read the Bible to them, especially the prophet Isaiah and the passages that spoke of the Lord's requirements that the oppressed should be freed and their burdens untied (e.g. Isa. 58:6–14).

The instruction that Josephine received from both her parents proved more durable than her weekly trips to the local parish church. The services were endured dutifully but she was more readily drawn to simple Methodist worship and the revivalist preaching that spoke of the Second Coming of Christ, when he would judge the world and reign in glory as king. It was the Christianity set forth in the Gospels that claimed her allegiance, and she would forever be captivated by the person of Christ. She had an enquiring mind but found, to her disappointment, that the clergy had no adequate answers to her deepest questions. She was frequently distressed by the extent of innocent suffering in the world. A visit she made to Ireland in 1847 at the height of the potato famine revealed scenes of poverty that were never erased from her mind. The sight of so much human misery and the shouts and wails of those in the final stages of their wretched existence prompted a religious crisis in her soul.

Towards the end of her life, in a letter to close friends, she confided for the first time that the inequalities and injustices she had seen all around her, had made her run into the woods close to her home. There, kneeling on the ground alone, she would pray directly to God, asking for deliverance for those who had no share in the world's banquet. Faith became 'a matter of life and death' to her. She wanted to be of use to God and, like the Psalmist,[1] she longed to know at first hand something of his truth and holiness.

Josephine was growing spiritually with a level of intensity that her sisters occasionally found disconcerting. There is nothing, however, to suggest that her religion made her less attractive or interesting as a person. She had little time or appetite for the conventional Christian piety that expected deference and restraint in women, and she was developing opinions of her own. She was also young and beautiful, dancing all night at local balls, turning heads with her white muslin frocks and the natural flowers in her hair. She loved the outdoors and became a skilful rider, with a great and abiding love of horses that she shared with her father.

Home life brought her happiness, and at her brother's graduation ceremony at Durham University on 6 February 1849, she met the new Classics master, George Butler. Within a year he was composing love poems for her. Three years later they were married: Josephine made a lovely bride with a white-and-orange wreath and a long veil. The parish church at Corbridge was full and five carriages made up the wedding procession.

In her new husband she found a partner nine years her senior, blessed with a fine academic mind. He was a keen sportsman who liked to start the day with a cold bath and a brisk walk and, if called upon, he could clear a five-bar gate with ease. George was also handsome, kind and humorous, with none of the intellectual arrogance or superiority that characterised some of his university peers. Despite their difference in age and an initial tendency on Josephine's part to look to him as her moral mentor, he was adamant that the marriage should be 'a perfectly equal union, with absolute freedom on both sides for personal initiative in thought and action and for individual development'.[2]

He was a deeply religious man who, like Josephine, had a suspicion of parsons. His vocation lay in teaching, but following protracted appeals from his father to take holy orders, George was ordained by the Bishop of Oxford in 1854 in a service that lasted almost four hours. Josephine noted later that 'when the bishop's hands rested on his shining curls I felt as if I was being ordained too'.[3] On the lips of another, such sentiments might appear cloying or presumptuous, but not in this instance. They testified to an extraordinary partnership and a meeting of minds and hearts that would leave an indelible mark on the nineteenth century.

Josephine and George had moved to Oxford following their marriage in 1852. The early years proved productive: George's reputation as an innovatory university teacher grew; at night they studied Italian together and prepared a new version of Chaucer's poems for publication. A first child was born – another George – but the new arrival did not prevent the musical evenings where Josephine performed Mozart and Beethoven quartets to appreciative gatherings, or the horse-riding trips to nearby Abingdon Park on summer nights to hear the nightingales. On the surface they were part of a pleasant, stimulating and agreeable society. But there was a shadow side. Increasingly, Josephine had to endure conversations and opinions that, for all their supposed brilliance, were actually myopic or condescending, particularly with regard to women. For a while she listened in silence but without sympathy. Eventually, however, she began to remonstrate openly when confronted with harmful prejudices or the double standard that allowed Victorian gentlemen (including Oxford dons) to take their sexual pleasures with prostitutes and then ignore or despise them afterwards.

It is possible to see here the first glimmer of the shared cause that would lead Josephine, with George in full support, to wage war on behalf of women and the poor. Their home was opened to the destitute. Much to the annoyance of disapproving onlookers but entirely in keeping with the example of Christ, she began to work with the social outcasts that refined Oxford society studiously ignored. Her health suffered. She wanted to do more for God but she was pregnant with her third child and there were bouts of anxiety and depression. Oxford was proving injurious to her well-being. Winter floods made the city cold and damp, and there was an awful smell in the meadows as the waters receded. Following medical advice, they moved to Cheltenham where George became College Vice-Principal. The job came with a large house that, in 1864, would become the scene of a domestic and personal tragedy from which Josephine never fully recovered.

On the afternoon of 20 August Josephine's daughter

Eva came to her to ask for a box in which to keep a caterpillar that she had found in the garden. Josephine obliged and sent her off to play. She never saw Eva again until George picked up her body later that evening. She had fallen from the banister at the top of the stairs. She remained unconscious for three hours and then died. She was five years old and her sudden death took possession of Josephine's mind and heart. For many years she never woke from sleep without the memory of the accident, and it was almost three decades before she could write about Eva's death. Josephine and George suffered like all bereaved parents, but they found consolation in their faith. The awful times when Josephine could not bear to visit the grave or attend church were tempered by a trust in God's loving purpose and an even deeper desire on her part to use her grief as a way of identifying with the 'poor groaning world' where so many young and innocent lives were cut short.

The opportunity to do this came in 1866 when George became the new headmaster of Liverpool College – a large school filled with almost 900 boys representing a variety of races and religions. He soon made his mark, and under his direction the college acquired a national reputation. Initially Josephine struggled. She had been desperately ill before leaving Cheltenham and depression followed her to Liverpool. Thoughts of Eva punctuated her waking hours and even her beloved piano remained unplayed. The desire to seek out human misery, however, and to do something about it had not died. She became involved with the Brownlow Hill Workhouse in the centre of Liverpool, a forlorn and desperate institution that housed up to 5000 inmates, including paupers, convicts, unmarried mothers and prostitutes. It was a place where hope was abandoned and a last refuge for the losers, nobodies and nuisances whom not even charitable refuges would entertain. Josephine acted differently: she talked to prostitutes with kindness and courtesy and found many of them homes. Eventually, with the help of generous Liverpool merchants and supportive friends, she established her own refuge, the Butlers' 'House of Rest', where residents who were not dying regained their health and dignity by sewing, laundering or making envelopes for local firms. They could earn sixpence a day, and women who had been in danger of resorting to prostitution through poverty received a second chance to remake their lives.

On the surface, it could appear that such Christian charity represented nothing more than the work of many refined English ladies who ministered to the poor of their parishes as part of their religious duties. But with Josephine it was different. She did not demean or judge the women whom she took from the workhouse, nor did she insist on their moral reform before she gave them renewed hope. Some of her evangelical contemporaries hedged their endeavours with stipulations or rules that were needlessly severe and therefore lacking the genuine compassion that asks only for the opportunity to serve others. At the inaugural service for the House of Rest, George Butler delivered no sermon and demanded no account of residents' past lives. With the tact and sympathy that endeared him to all those he taught, he read instead from the Gospel of Matthew, 'Come to me, all ye that labour and are heavy laden and I will give you rest' (11:28). His fledgling congregation received assurance and comfort, and before long many other lost souls came seeking sanctuary as Josephine's name became known amongst the destitute of the city.

Her empathy with 'Christ's poor' was remarkable. Before the House of Rest was established, she had brought girls from the street into her own home where they lived as valued guests, their chatter sometimes masking their consumptive coughing and their incredulity that such a fine place could be theirs. In Josephine and George they saw something of the love of God that they had never known before. If their lives proved short, they died with dignity and peace. One guest, Mary Lomax, stayed for three months and became like another sister to Josephine. They had met at Brownlow Hill where Mary had tried to poison herself after being thrown onto the streets coughing and spitting up blood. Josephine was unable to restore Mary's health but when she died, Josephine dressed the coffin and placed camellias around the frail body that had been violated from the age of fourteen. George officiated at the funeral service and Mary was buried in a plot adjoining a Butler family grave as a gesture of solidarity with the cause of the poor. A conviction was growing in Josephine that her calling was taking her beyond compassion and the care of souls to engage in a struggle against the evils of prostitution in the defence of women's civil and legal rights. Scorn, derision and political machinations of the very worst kind would lurk behind every corner, but she had faith and courage in abundance and the iron resolution that she would be heard.

She began to write and campaign for the better education of women and fairer wages for their work. Against the received wisdom that women should be paid less than men or that their only fitting career option was marriage, she spoke out on behalf of the vast numbers of spinsters and widows facing hardship or prostitution because they had no economic status in 'the great world's market' and were more often left 'cringing for a piece of bread'.[4] Against the presumption of motherhood, kitchen and home as the proper calling of women, she asked where that left the two and a half million single women for whom there were not enough husbands to go round. The reforming zeal of her father had entered her soul. Shortly before he died, he signed at her request a petition in support of protection for married women's property and earnings. He also added 'JP' after his name in the hope that, as an old magistrate, his signature would carry more weight.

By this time Josephine had been elected as the President of the North of England Council for the Higher Education of Women. For the first time, through a series of lectures delivered in nine Northern towns, women were encouraged to turn their eyes from needlework and domestic duties to the pursuit of science, maths, history, literature and international politics. This 'peripatetic university', staffed by talented university teachers, with George Butler providing academic support, drew over 500 students. Town libraries were required to equip their bookshelves with new stock to meet the requirements of these young women who knew they could be more than domestic goddesses.

Josephine was also finding her voice as a writer. Her first published article, *The Education and Employment of Women*, was followed by *Woman's Work and Woman's Culture*. She travelled to Cambridge to persuade the Senate to allow women to study there and to establish a college exclusively for women. The petition that she presented included the signatures of Florence Nightingale, Mrs Gladstone and Mrs Tennyson. The toil and travel, however, began to weaken her: at Cambridge she suffered from neuralgia and headaches, spending hours alone in a darkened room between lengthy interviews and meetings. Back in Liverpool, she slept in a separate bedroom from George because of her persistent coughing. She came close to choking through the amount of phlegm and blood, and only an open window and cold air brought her relief. Her tasks had multiplied: along with the work of the Council, there was the House of Rest, the visits to the workhouse and her political campaigning. But despite the tiredness that brought her to a low ebb, she knew that the divine spark had not deserted her and that to be in the presence of God for just one hour refreshed her more than sleep or anything else.

Much as she valued her educational activities, they were to cease by 1871 when she resigned as President of the North of England Council. Something had emerged from the shadows that she came to describe as 'this work of darkness' – an injustice so vile and cruel in its operations that, if it were left unchallenged, the important work of securing educational opportunities for women would be akin to 'building a beautiful house on top of a bad drain or upon a malarial swamp'.[5] God was calling her to new work, so shocking and fearful in its social and political implications that she trembled and her pillow became wet with tears.

Parliament had sanctioned 'a great wickedness', passing legislation that placed prostitutes in the hands of a special police in order to be subjected to medical procedures that treated such women as little more than 'ticketed human flesh' and attacked their civil rights. It was Josephine's hour – the mission she had dimly anticipated many years before, but seemingly 'afar off like a bright star'. Now it was her destiny to lead a public and political campaign to repeal an act that ostensibly regulated vice but enslaved women in the process. Friends and medical men urged her to take up the work, but it was many weeks before she could bring herself to raise the matter with George. A great deal was at stake for both of them, and as she finally approached his study, she still hesitated before handing him the written note that would shape their future. He grew pale and troubled in her presence and remained silent for several days. He knew the danger she would be subjected to and the detrimental effect on his own career and social standing. But he gave her his blessing and remained her staunchest supporter.

This is a good moment to pause in the story. We need to understand a little more concerning the background that led to the legislation that so enraged Josephine. Some imagination is also called for on our part to appreciate fully the enormity of what she was about to undertake and the opposition that was to follow.

The Contagious Diseases Act had first been introduced in 1864. Josephine was at that point lost to the world through her grief over Eva. Later she was to learn that Florence Nightingale had tried unsuccessfully to ban the legislation. In essence, its aim was to adopt the European system of licensed prostitution. Created initially to help curb the spread of syphilis and venereal diseases among the armed forces, the Act granted power to magistrates to order the genital examination of prostitutes and detain them for up to three months in degrading 'lock hospitals' until they were cured. It proved to be a system which '*hardened* women, confirmed them in their prostitution and condemned them to it'.[6] It also received the active support of politicians, national church leaders and parts of the medical profession. In some instances, doctors wanted to see the legislation extended to cover all major cities (whether they had military garrisons or not) or even the *entire* civil population. Prostitutes were regarded as little more than sewers and, in the interests of moral hygiene, they needed to be kept clean. All other considerations were secondary. It did not matter, on medical grounds, that the internal examination was frequently excruciating and demeaning. Here is one first-hand account of the procedure:

> It is awful work; the attitude they push us into first is so disgusting and so painful, and then these monstrous instruments – often they use several. They seem to tear the passage open first with their hands, and examine us, and then they thrust in instruments, and they pull them out and they push them in, and they turn and twist them about; and if you cry out they stifle you.[7]

If few in authority were concerned by the distress caused through this procedure, fewer still had thought about the moral dimension of an examination that came perilously close to rape. There was evidence to show that doctors in some instances took an inordinate amount of time over a procedure that was meant to be straightforward. There was also the enticement of lust and the opportunity to interfere with women that amounted to a form of surgical violation.

Josephine was familiar with and endorsed the medical and moral objections to the Act, but it was the *constitutional* violation of personal liberty on which she made her stand and her reputation. She quoted Magna Carta, warned that the political freedom of the nation rested on the preservation of the rights of all and challenged the fact that a suspected woman could be examined on the word of a police officer and a magistrate with no further procedures deemed necessary. Any other apprehended criminal was advised not to say anything which might incriminate him. On the other hand, women merely suspected of prostitution were required to sign forms, often under threat, that immediately and effectively handed their bodies over to an examining surgeon. Josephine argued that the legislation persecuted working-class women and campaigned for 'an equal code of morality, *one* standard for men and for women alike, equal laws based upon an equal standard'.[8] The precious principle of human liberty was at stake, along with the precarious and forlorn lives of many thousands of women driven into prostitution through social or economic necessity. But these were facts that polite Victorian society chose largely to ignore. Respectable men and women had other things to talk about in their drawing-rooms: prostitution and its causes was not one of them. It fell to Josephine to disturb their measured conversations.

Between June 1869 and June 1870, she addressed 99 public meetings and 4 conferences and travelled almost 4000 miles. As the head of the newly formed Ladies' National Association for the Repeal of the Contagious Diseases Act (the LNA), she moved through major towns and cities – Crewe, Leeds, York, Sunderland, Newcastle – often addressing large audiences of mainly working-class men who had never before heard political oratory from a woman. In her new role as a public speaker, she felt deep apprehensions concerning what she would say and how her controversial message would be received. In many instances she was heard gladly and her listeners were captivated by a gentle voice that nevertheless spoke with passion and resolve. She addressed working men as her brothers and genuinely felt this to be the case. She told them that 'two pence is the price in England of a poor girl's honour' and that legislation which perpetrated the lie that fallen women were utterly lost and worthless was a 'blasphemy against human nature and against God'. There were frequent bursts of applause and unsentimental men were visibly moved.

Unlike the roving politician of today, with the same remorseless message and soundbites for every audience, Josephine rarely repeated herself. Her words rang true because they were deeply felt and delivered with imagination and intelligence. She claimed hearts and minds because she was clear concerning central principles and extremely well briefed in the marshalling of her evidence and arguments. How she conducted such an arduous campaign is remarkable in itself. Her constitution was not strong and there was the frequent separation from George that both found hard. 'Be sure to let me know if you are not well', he wrote, 'and I will fly to you at once.'

In addition to the public meetings, petitions and protests were organised. The LNA began to collect signatures for their manifesto against the legislation and on 31 December 1869 it was published in the *Daily News*. It was a historic document, written by women to defend the rights of women. The House of Commons was perplexed and shaken: the revolt of women was a new thing and MPs were unsure as to how they should handle such opposition. Josephine's supporters saw in the manifesto a trumpet-call; supporters of the Contagious Diseases Acts greeted it with anger and abuse. Parts of the press turned on the LNA, accusing its members of being ridiculous or hysterical in turn. Josephine suffered many personal attacks on her character and marriage and was shunned in public. She also encountered great danger. In October 1870 at a by-election in Colchester the LNA put up a candidate against Sir Henry Storks, a keen advocate of the Acts. The LNA knew its candidate could not win but the aim was to split the vote to stop Storks from winning. Josephine was enlisted in support but few could have anticipated what would follow.

Dr J. Baxter Longley, a radical lawyer, had accepted the invitation to stand for the LNA. A brave man, he was not initially deterred by the personal threats he received via an organised campaign orchestrated by Storks' committee. At a repeal meeting in the town's theatre, his speech was drowned out by his audience and chairs, rotten vegetables and lumps of plaster from the ceiling were thrown at him. A police guard had to escort him to nearby lodgings where Josephine tended his bleeding face with lint and bandages. Outside a mob gathered. A window was smashed and stones were thrown into the room.

The next evening Josephine was due to address a large meeting for women only. Supporters urged her to cancel the event because Storks' 'bully boys' had posted her exact description on the walls of the town so that she would be recognised and mobbed. Resorting to disguise, she inveigled herself into the meeting, and after speaking had to escape through a back window, such was the din outside. During the two weeks of the election campaign, Josephine was repeatedly ejected from lodging houses, once her identity became known, and prayer meetings were routinely disturbed by street gangs.

On another occasion, in a later by-election in Pontefract during 1871, a fire was started beneath the room in which she was speaking: 'a smell of burning was felt, smoke began to curl up through the floor and a threatening noise was then heard underneath the door'.[9] Angry men were ready to 'kick her head' but local police officers arriving on the scene (Metropolitans hired by the Government) made no attempt to save her. She managed to escape and, amazingly, spoke later that evening in a hotel crowded with women. The lights were turned low for fear of the mob. Josephine recalled later in a memoir that 'we scarcely needed to speak – events had spoken for us, and all honest hearts were won'.[10]

The Colchester election proved a turning-point in the history of the crusade against the Acts. Storks was defeated. Josephine accepted advice to stay away on the day of the vote. Back home in Liverpool with her family, she received a telegram with the coded message, 'Shot dead'. The press agreed that Storks had been shot down – 'defeated by Mrs Josephine Butler'. The LNA rejoiced and looked to a future that now seemed full of hope.

The Government responded to the public controversy by setting up a Royal Commission. Some concessions were made – it proposed that the age of consent for girls be raised from 12 to 14 – but the possibility of outright repeal of the Acts was still a long way off. In fact it was much further down the road than Josephine or her supporters could have anticipated. It would be another sixteen years before her mission was accomplished. During this period over 900 public meetings were organised, 520 books and pamphlets on prostitution were published, and over 17,000 petitions with over 2 million signatures were published. One petition, pasted together on sheets, stretched for five miles and it took three men to hoist it onto the top of a cab before Josephine delivered it to Parliament. Many MPs laughed in derision but she continued to study and pray and learned to bear the delays and disappointments. Great acts take time and she was prepared to take the long view.

She also needed to rest if the work was to continue. A holiday in Switzerland with George, paid for by fellow workers, provided some respite and renewal. It was not long, however, before her campaign extended to the Continent where similar systems for regulating prostitution existed, with the same pernicious effects. In Switzerland, France and Italy she spoke tirelessly and with some success. Doors opened to her and influential contacts were made. She also witnessed scenes in prisons where prostitutes were held without trial that proved so distressing that she was unable to write about what she had seen. Worse still, she became aware of the extent of child prostitution on the Continent – the slave trade in English minors, mostly girls, who were abducted and imprisoned in foreign brothels and subjected to perversions and cruelties. It was five years before she felt able to speak about this white slave trade – 'innocent creatures, stolen, kidnapped, betrayed, got from English county villages by every artifice' – and then shipped abroad to endure a hell on earth at the hands of (mostly) wealthy and respectable men.

Through her tenacity and persistence, Parliament and then the wider community became aware of the grooming and abuse of domestic servants and maids and the recruitment of young girls for the brothels of Brussels, Antwerp and Paris. The king of Belgium alone bought around 100 virgins a year. Josephine knew that the key to stopping this white slave trade was to secure the legislation (scuppered on several previous occasions in the House of Commons) that would raise the age of consent from 13 to 16.

In a way that is hard to exaggerate and moving to

record, she brought about a revolution in the minds of people – especially the urban working class – that forced Parliament in 1885 to push through the Criminal Law Amendment Act that raised the age of consent to 16 (the same law we have today) and made it a criminal offence to procure girls for prostitution by threats, fraud or administering drugs. Less than a year later the Contagious Diseases Acts were also repealed. After the years of conflict, sorrows and disappointment and much fasting and prayer, a vindictive and worthless Act of Parliament was erased from the constitution and the nation recognised the system of regulation for what it was: 'arbitrary, unjust and cruel to the women concerned'.[11]

Although this represented the culminating triumph of Josephine's life, she showed no inclination to stand still or slow down. George had been made a canon of Winchester Cathedral, and within a short time following his appointment, she had established a new House of Rest just a few minutes' walk from the Cathedral Close. Its purpose was to serve as a hospital and a temporary home for mature women and girls who were 'friendless, betrayed and ruined'[12] and beyond the scope of more respectable hostels. She sat lightly to the worshipping life of the Cathedral and increasingly found it necessary to give more time and support to George. He was by now a sick man who felt a keen disappointment that he had been unable to achieve very much during his ministry at the Cathedral. He died in a London hotel on 13 March 1890. Josephine took a lock of his hair and placed it in a case that she carried constantly. She was sixty-two when he died and they had been married for thirty-eight years. Less than two years later she had written his biography as a testimony to their 'united life' and his goodness.

His death proved a great trial to her and she was to outlive him by sixteen years. She moved home several times, living with her sister and then with each of her three sons. She had to contend with insomnia, her own declining health and months of extreme pain. She withdrew from public life but remained a great letter-writer and took pleasure in the company of her grandchildren. She declined to be photographed because previous attempts had shown an expression of melancholy and suffering that misrepresented her character. She resolved to 'die without any fuss'. At 5 a.m. on Sunday, 30 December 1906 she thanked her nurse for her care, whispered her last prayer and then, two hours later, died peacefully. She was buried at a small church in Kirknewton, Northumberland on 3 January 1907. There were no public demonstrations of mourning for her death – the world, as ever, was too busy to dwell overmuch on her great achievements some twenty years before – but the newspapers were gracious in their estimations:

> Mrs Butler's name will always rank amongst the noblest of those social reformers the fruit of whose labours is the highest inheritance that we have. She fought with enormous courage and self-sacrifice in a battlefield where she was subjected to the fiercest antagonism and the most distressing aspects of life that a delicately nurtured woman could be brought into contact with. She never faltered in her task, and it is to her in supreme that the English Statute Book owes the removal of one of the grossest blots that ever defaced it. Her victory marked one of the greatest stages in the progress of woman to that

equality of treatment which is the final test of a nation's civilization.[13]

The obituary notice was headed 'A Noble Woman'. A century later there are no grounds for revising or questioning the title. In keeping with the more brave and enterprising pilgrims of past generations who surrendered their lives to Christ, she was sometimes guilty of the sin of 'gross mismanagement of herself, attempting the impossible ... and assuming that excellence of purpose can atone for neglect of the laws of health'.[14] The only fault a contemporary could find in her was the extravagance that had once led Josephine to place expensive flowers in the coffin of the prostitute Mary Lomax who, we recall, died of consumption at the Butler house on a cold, snowy March day. Far from being extravagant, others (myself included) will interpret this final gesture as evidence that Josephine practised at first hand the gospel generosity that is particularly reserved for the prodigal and the lost. We are not surprised to learn that dying prostitutes saw something of Christ in the face of Josephine, for in a way that few ever manage, she gave her full obedience to his character and commands.

For reflection

From this opening chapter, how does Josephine emerge as a woman of faith and action? What distinguishes her from her contemporaries in terms of 'good works' and concern for the poor?

Her father John Grey imparted to her a strong sense of social justice derived from his reading of the Old Testament prophets. Read the following passage:

Seek good and not evil, that you may live; and so the Lord, the God of hosts will be with you, just as you have said. Hate evil and love good and establish justice in the gate … let justice roll down like waters, and righteousness like an ever flowing stream … Hear this you who trample on the needy, and bring ruin to the poor of the land saying, 'When will the new moon be over so that we may sell grain; and the sabbath so that we may offer wheat for sale? Who will make the ephah smell and the shekel great and practise deceit with false balances, buying the poor for silver, and the needy for a pair of sandals, and selling the sweepings of the wheat?' The Lord has sworn by the pride of Jacob: Surely I will never forget any of their deeds.

(Amos 5:14–15, 24; 8:4–7)

To what extent does our reading of the Old Testament still continue to inform and shape our beliefs and actions? Can we say where the difference lies between the pursuit of social justice and practical compassion? In our experience, do we find ourselves more easily drawn to one than the other? Can we say why?

Read the following passage:

When he came to Nazareth, where he had been brought up, he went to the synagogue on the sabbath day, as was his custom. He stood up to read, and the scroll of the prophet Isaiah was given to him. He unrolled the scroll and found the place where it was written:

'The Spirit of the Lord is upon me because he has anointed me to bring good news to the poor. He has sent me to proclaim release to the captives and recovery of sight for the blind, to let the oppressed go free, to proclaim the year of the Lord's favour.'

And he rolled up the scroll, gave it back to the attendant and sat down. The eyes of all the synagogue were fixed on him. Then he began to say to them, 'Today this scripture has been fulfilled in your hearing.'

(Luke 4:16–21)

It seems clear from this reading that Jesus was driven by 'the great cause' of the Kingdom of God. For Josephine this amounted to the repeal of unjust legislation and renewed hope and freedom for brutalised women. What great cause or causes does the gospel require us to embrace today?

To ponder

'When Christ calls a man,' says Dietrich Bonhoeffer, 'he bids him come and die.' There are different kinds of dying, it is true; but the essence of discipleship is contained in those words.

G. K. A. Bell, late Bishop of Chichester

- Do we agree that this represents the heart of the matter for Christianity?
- From Josephine's life, what are the pitfalls and dangers of such a radical form of discipleship?
- How can we avoid them without resorting to soft options?

To pray

Since today is a new day I will begin again
With Jesus Christ, my Lord.

Bob Knight

Give us
A pure heart
That we may see Thee,
A humble heart
That we may hear Thee,
A heart of love
That we may serve Thee
A heart of faith
That we may live Thee,
Thou whom I do not know
But whose I am.

Dag Hammarskjold (1905–61)

O my God, I have no idea where I am going. I do not
see the road ahead of me. Nor do I really know
myself, and the fact that I think I am following your
will does not mean that I am actually doing so. But I
desire to do your will, and I know the very desire
pleases you. Therefore I will trust you always though
I may seem lost. I will not fear, for you are always
with me, O my dear God.

Thomas Merton (1915–68)

Holy Spirit, coming so silently,
giving life and refreshment and beauty everywhere;
coming in a way none can understand;
coming invisibly;
coming in the night of affliction;

may your peace dwell in my heart,
may your strength invigorate me,
may your love kindle my whole being,
to love him who first loved me.
Lord, whatever kind of person I am,
I am always yours.

J. M. Neale (1818–66)

Chapter 2

PRAYER, PASSION AND THE INNER LIFE

I N MANY WAYS JOSEPHINE Butler was an unconventional Christian. No church ever claimed her complete allegiance and she showed little interest in religious dogma or the doctrinal controversies of her day.[1] She valued Cathedral services at Winchester for the opportunity they gave her for uninterrupted contemplation, but she disliked intensely the dark shadow of institutional Christianity when it failed the neglected poor. She was, however, drawn to the Christian past and felt a deep attraction to the saints – those 'who shone like bright stars in a dark sky' and in times of tyranny 'lived near to God and taught his love'. Teresa of Avila[2] became one of her favourite authors and her famous work *The Life of Prayer* set Josephine on a new path. She also venerated Francis of Assisi and Catherine of Siena.[3] For Josephine, the saints made God real and their lives contained a secret known only to those who followed Christ as the vital source of their hope and identity. The secret was bound up with a hidden life of prayer that was offered with the whole of their being for the sake of the world. At great personal cost and with no thought of material reward, they fashioned an inner life that generated love for the stranger and justice for the persecuted. That Josephine understood all this and was inspired by such great lives can be explained by the fact that her work as a formidable social reformer was grounded in prayer. She prayed 'without ceasing',[4] often under intolerable pressure but never as a special activity removed from the rest of her life. Sometimes her conversations with God broke her heart and on other occasions constituted a great peace. Prayer, in her own words, was a case of *wrestling* or *resting*, and to the end of her life she retained the practice, even when she had been 'set aside from the battle' and could no longer hold a pen.

In her earlier years and particularly through the long struggle to repeal the Contagious Diseases Act, she practised the costly work of intercession, bringing before God the needs of the outcast and unloved. It showed in her face. Here is a famous description of Josephine recorded in the writings of Canon Henry Scott Holland[5] as he glimpsed her through a carriage window at the height of her campaign:

> About twenty-eight years ago, in passing up Holborn, a face looked at me out of a hurrying hansom, which arrested and frightened me. It was framed on pure and noble and beautiful lines: but it was smitten, and bitten into, as by some East wind, that blighted it into a grey sadness. It had seen that which took all colour and joy out of it. I felt as the children who saw Dante pass as a shadow through the sunny square: and whispered 'He has been in Hell'. The face had a look, I thought, of recognition before it had swiftly gone: and, after I had recovered my memory, I knew that it was Josephine Butler. A day

or two later, a message reached me from her, to warn me that a tremendous storm was about to break, and that all the friends of the Cause must be prepared for the emergency ... and then, I knew that I had seen, that day in Holborn, Mrs Butler in the thick of that terrible work that she has undertaken for God. She was passing through her martyrdom. The splendid beauty of her face, so spiritual in its high and clear outlines, bore the mark of that death upon it to which she stood daily and hourly committed. There was no hell on earth into which she would not willingly travel, if, by sacrifice of herself, she could reach a hand of help to those poor children whom nothing short of such sacrifice could touch. The sorrow of it passed into her being. She had the look of the world's grim tragedy in her eyes. She had dared to take the measure of the black infamy of sin: and the terrible knowledge had left its cruel mark upon the soul of strange and singular purity.[6]

It is a moving and powerful image, reminding us that the heart of the gospel is never far removed from tragedy. Christians are called to be 'burden bearers'[7] and the redemption of the earth is bound up with our readiness to embrace the violence, horror and hatred of our time. To an uncomfortable degree, the world shapes our agenda and requires us to work and pray with the Psalmist that 'the needy shall not always be forgotten nor shall the hope of the poor perish for ever'.[8] Josephine saw the world through Christ's eyes and heard with terrible acuity what Wordsworth called 'the still, sad music of humanity'. She suffered without ever despairing because her life was 'hidden with Christ in God' (Col. 3:3) and there was for her no evil in the world that could not be met with 'a corresponding beauty and glory'.[9]

The word 'beauty' has some bearing here on her personality. Some readers might already be tempted to view Josephine as a Victorian 'iron lady' – feared and respected for her indomitable will and high purpose but possibly never actually loved because of her single-mindedness that sometimes created enemies. There are recorded occasions where she lacked diplomacy or delicacy of touch, but this could hardly have been otherwise. She spent years 'swimming against the stream' and prophets are rarely associated with smooth words. This much conceded, however, the picture we have is that of a gracious woman who retained her humanity and influenced many by her example. Sometimes at Cambridge she would talk privately to more than forty undergraduates. The 'minute particulars' of other lives mattered to her. Minds were moulded by her, and Canon Scott Holland wrote in gratitude: 'few in this generation know the wonder and beauty and the power put out over men of her own day by the personal heroism of Josephine Butler'.[10]

Somehow she managed a very difficult juggling act. She didn't see herself as a visionary or dreamer and her practical nature meant that she was easily drawn to projects and causes rather than contemplation. Yet through discipline and what she described as 'the travail of soul' arising from her awareness of social injustice, she learnt to be still and made her desires known to God:

> I spoke to Him in solitude, as a person who could answer. I sometimes gave whole nights to prayer, because the day was not sufficiently my own. Do not imagine that on these occasions I worked myself up

into any excitement; there was much pain in such an
effort and dogged determination required. Nor was
it a sentimental devotion which urged me on. It was
a desire to know God and my relation to Him.[11]

Josephine gave herself over to prayer as a passionate and
loving form of *attention* both to God as the ultimate
spiritual force and source of righteousness beyond herself
and to the concerns that distressed her soul. She prayed
with energy and in her physical weakness was sent out and
made stronger. The hours of intercession made for some
mysterious alchemy within her: the divine spark fanned
into flame, her strength increased and her vision encom-
passed the wrongs that to others appeared invisible. Her
prayer became a matter of *seeing*. Josephine was able to
care for people indiscriminately and in their entirety
because she was alert to the pain of their existence. Prayer
induced in her an extraordinary empathy and intensity of
feeling, and what she felt constituted the knowledge that
led her to act.

As her campaign gained momentum, George Eliot was
writing *Middlemarch*, the greatest English novel of the
nineteenth century. Some of its most famous lines concern
themselves with the human duty to be alive to every shade
of human feeling and serious about our dependence on
each other. I cannot read these words without Josephine
coming to mind:

If we had a keen vision and feeling for all ordinary
human life, it would be like hearing the grass grow
and the squirrel's heart beat, and we should die of
that roar which lies on the other side of silence. As it
is, the quickest of us walk about well wadded with
stupidity.[12]

On the other side of silence, Josephine heard the roar of human traffic that represented broken lives and shattered dreams. She also heard the 'still small voice' that constituted her hope and strength in the long struggle to mend injustices. Her juggling act required her to hold two different kinds of activity together. Like Jesus, she travelled through towns and cities in active pursuit of the kingdom of purity and love. The public square became the domain where she contested ignorance, indifference and self-interest. But she also withdrew into solitude and, like her Lord and Master, found refreshment and perspective in detachment. She prayed in lonely places, sometimes before the sun rose (Mark 1:35), and sought the quietness of the hills (Mark 6:46). She would have understood well the wisdom of St Benedict[13] that the religious life is a constant movement between the desert and the marketplace and that both are needed for the journey of discipleship.

Two important truths begin to emerge at this point, one rather more subtle than the other. Before we explore them, a little more needs to be said about Josephine's story and her decision to write a biography of Catherine of Siena. The book appeared in 1878 and it is not difficult to see why Josephine was drawn to her subject.

Catherine lived from 1347 to 1380, a demoralising time for the people of Italy when political corruption was rife and the Church was inducing despondency amongst the faithful. Its morals had become lax; the lives of its prelates gave rise to scandal and, most disastrous of all, a Pope residing in France was neglecting the needs of his Italian subjects.[14] Intrigues of various kinds seemed the order of the day; earthly success was vaunted as the only criterion of human achievement, and the call to sacrifice and service, first heard by Simon and Andrew as they fished the waters of Galilee, was barely audible above the din of a Church that was knee deep in dishonour. Josephine wrote:

> The voluntary exile of the Pope ... had a most melancholy effect upon the faith, the morals and the politics of the Church. The corruption of the pre-lates, the dishonourable and scandalous lives of the young cardinals, and the universal licence of the city were so notorious to all Europe, that Avignon received the name of the 'Western Babylon'.[15]

Into this mire came Catherine, born on the Feast of the Annunciation and from an early age destined to lead a religious life that would take her from the confines of a private room to the corridors of the Papacy. Barely twenty and after three years of prayer and study during which she desired above all else to do the will of Christ, she embarked on a ministry of reconciliation. Her reputation for holiness grew and many amended their lives under her influence. Her greatest achievement was to persuade Pope Gregory XI to leave Avignon (despite the opposition of his French cardinals) and return to the Holy City. Imagine: none of the 'movers and shakers' of the age had been able to persuade or cajole Gregory into making such a move. His own advisers counselled against it and there was deep anger in regions of Italy against the Holy See on the part of those who, quite legitimately, felt abandoned by their chief pastor. An intractable and dangerous situation faced a young woman still not thirty and wearing only the black-and-white habit of the Dominican Order as her seal of service as she entered the gates of Avignon on 18 June 1376. She had written many letters to Gregory urging him to reconsider for the sake of peace and for the needs of his abandoned people. Now she stood before him: 'Fulfil what you have promised,' she asked – reminding him of a vow which he had never disclosed to any other person.[16] Extraordinarily, Gregory complied. Catherine went ahead to smooth the path. Not everyone had welcomed her intervention. She faced many dangers and swords were drawn against her. Two years after his return, Gregory died. His successor, Urban VI, sought out Catherine for advice and support. She became his trusted counsellor and finally took up residence in Rome where her prayers and encouragement sustained the Pope through turbulent and acrimonious times when, yet again, a rival Pope was established in Avignon by cardinals who had declared Urban's election illegal. In 1380 Catherine was paralysed by a stroke and on 29 April, at the age of thirty-three, she died. The wounds she had received as stigmata just five years earlier in the little church of St Christina after making her communion, became clearly visible after her death.[17] She was canonised in 1461 and in April 2000 became Patroness of Europe.

Timothy Radcliffe, who was Master of the Dominicans at the beginning of this new century, has written in praise of her prodigious energy that emerged from the depths of a contemplative faith:

> Catherine worked on two seemingly contradictory levels, a public level and a private level. She walked with Popes and had their ear on the international policy making but she also cultivated what she called 'a cell of self-knowledge'.[18]

Commenting on her ability to fuse her inner and outer lives to powerful effect, he continues:

Catherine of Siena offers a liberating answer to the contemporary quest for identity. It takes us far away from a false identity based on status, wealth and power. For at the heart of our being is the God whose love sustains us in being. This is the place of contemplative prayer, where one meets God who delights in loving and forgiving, and whose own goodness we taste. Here we discover the secret of Catherine's peace and her dynamism, her confidence and her humility. This is what made this young woman, with little formal education a great preacher. This is what gave her the freedom to speak and to listen. This is what gave her the courage to dive in and address the great issues of her time.[19]

In Catherine, Josephine Butler found a soul friend and advocate. Separated by centuries and important differences in the trajectories of their lives – one opting for monastic celibacy, the other, marriage and family – they forged a spiritual dynamic that reconciled the apparent opposites of private prayer and public action. Religion and politics were the great causes of their lives, with the latter arising out of the prayer and silence that were the preconditions of communion with God and the discernment of his ways. Josephine was adamant that prayer could never truly be called communion if the only voice heard was that of the intercessor. Stillness and attention were required once petitions had been brought to the throne of heaven, for then, and only then, could the voice of God be heard within, and with it 'the clearer vision of duty'.[20]

In their need of solitude and their frequent forays into the public arena, Catherine and Josephine point us to the truths that were alluded to earlier. In the first instance, passion of itself is never enough, even in the high cause of the kingdom. In a recent book about inner-city mission,[21] I noted how urban practitioners can sometimes be so pre-occupied with projects and pastoral care that there is neither space nor scope for prayer or the discernment of God's will. Two problems follow: excessive busyness can mask a form of witness that appears profound on the surface but actually, deep down, is rather superficial. In a serendipitous moment late last night when my thoughts were far removed from these pages, I came across the following observation and gave a nod of recognition as I read:

> And so it is that much of the current Christian activism seems to be a smoke screen for shallowness, for lack of roots, for the activist to hide the fact that he hasn't the foggiest notion of what he's about. He is, as he likes to say, 'the man for others'. And this is how it should be. But many are the activists today, who, when scratched only superficially, reveal only the vaguest notion of what it means to be 'for' anyone.[22]

With this lack of clarity and purpose can also come the danger of 'burn-out' through stress, disillusionment or weariness. There are never enough hours and everything becomes urgent. Consequently morale and vision grow dim and creative possibilities shrink. It is prayer and the time given only to God through withdrawal that can prevent Christian faith from turning into just one more form of social service and enable it to withstand the dis-appointments and failures that attend the pilgrim way. Solidarity with the forsaken, as Catherine and Josephine came to realise, can only be sustained over long periods by an equally passionate engagement with 'the silence beyond words, towards which all genuine praying moves'.[23]

A less obvious insight that can prevent our work and prayer from being skewed or our enthusiasm from being too easily dissipated has to do with the meaning of the scriptural injunction to 'pray without ceasing'. To put a difficult notion in its simplest terms, it amounts to this: prayer as a specific activity represents a normal and regular part of each day of anyone who, like the saints, genuinely aspires to be a friend of God. Within that framework, other duties, including work, are in some sense prayer – they proceed from the mind and heart that have already placed themselves before God in order to seek and do his will. But there is a caveat! Take away the framework and the disciplined pattern of prayer that upholds it, and the flattering notion that all life is prayer falls to the ground. Aelred Squire observes:

> For someone who never, or hardly ever prays, it is simply not true that his work is part of his prayer. It is manifestly, at best, a substitute for it and it could even be a refusal to take the trouble to have anything directly to do with the mystery of God, and so be a deliberate impoverishment of all that is most human in us.[24]

Josephine accepted no substitutes. She knew that she would perish if she ceased from prayer, and her persistence enabled other lives that had become withered to bloom again. She teaches us that prayer and passion go together, for our own sake and for our love of God's world in all its need and longings.

There is one more thing to say. Prayer is also about inner peace. Josephine wrestled in prayer for much of her life but she also rested. In the 'long revolution' that was her campaign, there were few days of miracle and wonder. Much of it was struggle and, to some extent, she expected no less. But there were also consolations. In silence, the noise of the world was momentarily stilled. In the great space of Winchester Cathedral she was able to breathe the air of heaven and glimpse angels' wings. And in her petitions to God, there sometimes came the words of Infinite Love that she experienced as a form of benediction: 'Peace, be still.' Confronted by the endless agitation that took its physical toll on her vulnerable frame, she never lost her sense of the divine. In old age, as she handed on her life's work to others, she wrote to a friend:

> He has brought me of late, nearer to Him than ever before; and He has given me an assurance such as I never had before, that all those I love and pray for are *safe* in His hands … Then a great hush came over my soul, a kind of *awe* in the Divine Presence. I was overpowered. I held out my hand and said, 'Take this weak hand into thy powerful hand' and I realised that He did. He took my hand in His and *promised* me He would hold it for ever, and that my prayer was safe with Him for ever.[25]

The roots of this sense of assurance went deep. Josephine's faith was a religion of the heart. God was indubitably real to her and she felt his presence 'on the pulse'. She trusted in his providential workings and longed above most things to be worthy of the name Christian. She knew that the genuinely good life was grounded in gratitude, and in prayer the frequent mercies of God became occasions of praise. In leaving the world, she gave thanks for all her days, the beauty of the setting sun, the precious trace of

memories and the support of those who had stood by
her side and furthered humanity. In such things and in her
prayerful devotion to Jesus in his passion, she found
her final peace.

For reflection

The following extracts are from the private diary of Dag
Hammarskjold, Secretary General of the United Nations
(published as *Markings* by Faber & Faber, 1964).

> Hallowed be Thy name
> *not mine,*
> Thy kingdom come,
> *not mine,*
> Thy will be done,
> *not mine,*
> Give us peace with Thee
> Peace with men
> Peace with ourselves,
> And free us from all fear.

> In the faith which is 'God's marriage to the soul',
>   you are *one* in God, and
> God is wholly in you,
> just as, for you, He is wholly in all you meet.
> With this faith, in prayer you descend into yourself
>   to meet the Other,
> in the steadfastness and light of this union,
> see that all things stand, like yourself, alone before
>   God,
> and that each of your acts is an act of creation,
>   conscious,

because you are a human being with human
   responsibilities,
but governed, nevertheless, by the power beyond
   human
consciousness which has created man.
You are liberated from things, but you encounter in
   them an experience which has the purity and
   clarity of revelation.
In the faith which is 'God's marriage to the soul',
   everything, therefore has a meaning.
So live, then, that you may use what has been put
   into your hand.

To have humility is to experience reality, not *in
relation to ourselves*, but in its sacred independence. It
is to see, judge, and act from the point of rest in
ourselves. Then, how much disappears, and all that
remains falls into place.

In the point of rest at the centre of our being, we
encounter a world where all things are at rest in the
same way. Then a tree becomes a mystery, a cloud, a
revelation, each man a cosmos of whose riches we
can only catch glimpses. The life of simplicity is
simple, but it opens to us a book in which we never
get beyond the first syllable.

- To what extent do these extracts illuminate Josephine's life and faith?
- What do they tell us about the road to personal
  freedom?

To ponder

Once we have grasped clearly what we are doing when we pray for others, we shall see that the most important requirement by far is inner calmness and tranquillity. We are not engaged in creating or producing anything, but in becoming aware of what is already the fact, namely that God is immediately and intimately present both to ourselves and to the ones for whom we are praying. Our task is to hold the awareness of this fact in the still centre of our being, to unite our love for them with God's love, in the quiet but total confidence that he will use our love to help bring about the good in them which we both desire. In technical terms, therefore, intercession is a form of that kind of prayer known as 'contemplation', with the special feature that here we contemplate not God himself but God in his relationship of love towards those whom we also love; and on the basis of our partnership with him we entrust our love into his hands to be used in harness with his own for their benefit.

From *The Foolishness of God* by John Austin Baker

To pray

He did not say, 'You shall not be tempest-tossed, you shall not be work-weary, you shall not be discomforted.' But he said, 'You shall not be overcome.' God wants us to heed these words so that we shall always be strong in trust, both in sorrow and in joy.

Mother Julian of Norwich

Teach us, O Father, to trust Thee with life and with
death,
And (though this is harder by far)
With the life and death of those that are dearer to us
than our life.

Teach us stillness and confident peace
In thy perfect will,
Deep calm of soul and content
In what Thou wilt do with these lives Thou hast given.

Teach us to wait and be still,
To rest in Thyself,
To hush the clamorous anxiety,
To lay in Thine arms all this wealth Thou hast given.

Thou lovest these souls that we love
With a love far surpassing our own
As the glory of noon surpasses the gleam of a candle.
Therefore will we be still,
And trust in Thee.

J. S. Hoyland

My hands will I lift up
unto Thy commandments which I have loved.
Open Thou mine eyes that I may see,
incline my heart that I may desire,
order my steps that I may follow,
the way of Thy commandments.
    O Lord God, be Thou to me a God,
    and beside Thee none else,
    none else, nought else with Thee.

Lancelot Andrewes

Chapter 3

REMEMBERING THE POOR: THE PASTORAL TASK

A CONFESSION TO BEGIN this third chapter: At the back of a book on my prayer desk, tucked away discreetly between the pages, I have a picture of Josephine Butler. Actually, there are two photographs there. The other is of George Butler. I find his benign gaze reassuring, particularly on those days when the priestly task leaves me feeling empty or frustrated. Josephine looks beautiful and assured in a way that belies how often she descended into hell as she fulfilled her destiny. I cherish both images. Josephine and George continue to speak to me across a century and more. They have become part of the furniture of my mind and, not infrequently, as I wrestle with pastoral or social issues, I find myself wondering how Josephine would react to such situations. I have not yet taken the devotional step of wearing a wrist-band with her name on it, but she has become a conversation partner and therefore inextricably linked with my own ministry and praying. In what follows I want to suggest why it is that she remains significant and relevant to anyone with more

than half a mind fixed on the unfinished task of being a
Christian.

In terms of her moral seriousness and compassion and
the searching range of her considerable intellect, she is a
living reminder that the gospel demands the best of us. In
her own words, it is 'deep, difficult and holy work'. Even
Jesus had to 'set his face towards Jerusalem' (Luke 9:51)
in order to fulfil its demands. Over the years this phrase –
'deep, difficult and holy work' – has insinuated itself into
my vocabulary. I don't use it in conversation or with
students, but I know it's there as a discrete part of my
religious grammar, subtly underpinning what I'm about.
Because I love words and recognise their power to shape
and change the way we see the world, the clever juxta-
position of 'deep', 'difficult' and 'holy' strikes me as the
craft of a woman who thought very carefully before her
pen touched the paper. By definition each of these words
represents a particular kind of profundity and expresses for
me Josephine's obedience of faith. She represents the cost
and conscience of authentic Christian witness and challenges us to embrace the gospel as a life-changing
experience. This is surely a timely word for us when a
good deal of what passes for true religion often amounts to
just one more comfortable life-style choice to enhance our
well-being or success.

Josephine does not flinch from the fact that Jesus makes
demands and in this matter she has no wish to be deceived.
Since the time of St Paul, others have said the same, but
sometimes with a burning intensity that few of us can heed
or hope to embrace. With Josephine, the intensity is
softened by her grace and beauty; by the gentleness of her
spirit in the face of human suffering; by her artistic talent
and creativity and her ability to smile and wonder. Her

religion is not confined to the canvas prescribed by the Church of her day. It is instead, as we have seen, a great cause, an adventure that claims heart and mind in equal measure, and an invitation to discern God's grandeur in the mysteries of his creation and the lives of the 'humble and meek'. Josephine's life is an extended Magnificat: her soul proclaims the greatness of the Lord, but with every means at her disposal she desires to lift up the lowly even if it means casting the mighty from their thrones. Her religion has the feel of poetry about it: she knows that life's immensities evade simple formulations of any kind, but she is also deeply conscious of the duty to act in an unequivocal way when justice is denied and the cries of the poor die on the wind. I recognise a toughness in her approach that might frighten some people off, but others – hopefully the readers of this book among their number! – will sense an obligation and summons that speak to our hunger to be more serious and our desire for depth in a floating world.

Part of the summons, in words of St Paul that Josephine would readily endorse, is to 'remember the poor' (Gal. 2:10). There are several references in the New Testament that reveal Paul as a diligent pastor organising a collection among the churches he founded to be sent to Jerusalem, possibly for food after the famine of AD 46/48. He is eager to do this work because he is committed to a Christ who is Son of *Man*. Paul's gospel of salvation is wonderfully inclusive. It is about preaching good news and the mysterious acts of God in Christ, but it is also rooted and grounded in the love that gives ever more of itself. Paul reaches out to the poor in the name of One who had nowhere to lay his head and was placed in a borrowed tomb. He asks that we give to those in need and extend hospitality to strangers (Rom. 12:13) as if they were Christ. And in his requests we can hear the echo of Jesus in Matthew's Gospel: 'for as much as you did it to one of the least of these you did it to me' (25:40).

We know a considerable amount about the poor of Josephine's day – the thousands who fell into a gulf of misery and ended their lives in workhouses separated from loved ones – and we have seen how she responded in such appalling circumstances to individuals who had lived on the streets or in fever-ridden tenements, well beyond the fold of organised religion. By this time, Wesley's Methodism had become the religion of the forgotten poor, with its itinerant preachers bringing relief to parishes where some Anglican clergy found the filth and stench unending and unbearable. As Josephine began her rescue mission at the Brownlow Hill Workhouse in Liverpool, it was a Baptist minister, Charles Birrell, who set her on her path and gave her advice based on his own regular visits to the work-house. We must assume that he had a generous pastoral heart and, despite the difficulty of the task, he at least knew who the poor were and where they were likely to be found.

In our own day, when we have become accustomed to ever higher standards of living, it is easy to forget that the scourges of poverty and human misery still blight the streets and roads of our unequal nation. The latest official statistics[1] show that child poverty has been rising again since 2004/5, and few city centres are free of those individuals whose plight we ignore or fail to comprehend. As Nicholas Holtam has noted in his recent book on the ministry of St Martin-in-the-Fields London,[2] most of us tend to look at poverty sideways. He observes that few of us rarely look at street beggars: 'we tend to be uncertain or embarrassed and look out of the corner of our eye'.[3]

As a supporter of *The Big Issue*, I also know that its street vendors often wish that buyers would actually engage them in a brief conversation instead of thrusting coins into their hands before hurriedly making off with the magazine. Selling *The Big Issue* is not just about survival. It is, for some, the first step to a renewed confidence or sense of self-worth that is made possible through a conversation (however brief) predicated on a shared humanity. Our sense of self, of who we are and what we amount to in the eyes of others, is for most of us precariously assembled and easily dismantled.

Holtam tells a story about one of his predecessors, Austen Williams, who was a good pastor and listener. Williams was dashing between the vicarage and the church one day when a man stopped him.

'Remember me?' said the stranger.

Williams, late and flustered, asked, 'How much do you want?'

'I only wanted to know that you remember me,' the man replied, evidently crushed.[4]

I can identify with the tale and the embarrassed cleric. Like St Martin's, my own parish church here in the centre of Southport is open each day. People come through our doors to be quiet, to light a candle, to weep for a loved one, to pray for a departed soul, to be helped out of a mess. Some are badly damaged and, occasionally, deranged. There is no immediate or obvious pastoral response to the woman who insists that she has been made pregnant by King George III, or the man who hands me an unintelligible manuscript with the severe warning that he is Jesus Christ and I must read it before the world ends a few days hence, or the young lady with Satan in her head who has no wish for him to be there.

And it has to be said that there is no shortage of people who are difficult and demanding because they have fallen down through various addictions, abusive or broken relationships, loss of work or just bad luck. In consequence, they have ceased to keep diaries, carry no watch and are spectacularly free of engagements, except the encounters that keep them alive or, at least, existing. They do things differently and sometimes, on my part, a service, a funeral or the next appointment gets in the way of any genuine response. I give them cash to ease my schedule but what they sometimes want or need is my time.

As I am writing these words, B has just come to the door with an electronic tag on his leg and 22 prison sentences to his name. He is barely 30 with a history of violence, yet he is always affable when he comes to me. We strike a deal fairly quickly in this instance and he goes away happy.

Many years ago I lost an altar server because he saw me turn away a man at the vestry door just as the main Sunday service was about to begin, with a congregation primed to lift up their hearts. I hope the server has forgiven me by now and come to realise that sometimes clergy have to make lousy choices when competing needs collide.

Remembering the poor is an unsettling experience. The steady procession of those who live at the margins of society or believe they will never form part of it is never ending, and it is not always possible to see the face of Christ in the manipulative, the self-obsessed or the con-artist. But there are illuminations on the way: the human stories that humble, the promises to repay that are kept, the insights that come from lives that have no reputations to lose, the challenge to retain our humanity on the days when we are too busy for our own good. As Josephine

moved among the destitute in Liverpool, she never lost
sight of the importance of the individual. Her presence
was welcomed when clergy were sometimes spurned.
Perhaps they were too formal, perfunctory or barely able
to conceal their wish to be elsewhere – anywhere, in fact,
in preference to the darkness and disease of the workhouse. My sense is that Josephine took risks, remembered
to pray in the presence of suffering and was not afraid to
stand alongside the unloved in the conviction that 'no one
had spoken lovingly to them before'.[5] Because she desired
to be a friend of God, she became a friend to others,
offering them, first and foremost, her humanity that made
a deep and lasting impression. She knew how to be vulnerable as well as assured and did not assail the helpless
with an avalanche of words.

The poet Charles Causley wrote a memorable poem
about hospital visiting. In it he describes various kinds of
visitors, ranging from those who 'destroy hope in the
breasts of the sick' to the remorseless banter and weak
jokes, 'menacing as shell splinters', of the son attempting
to cheer his aged mother:

> 'They'll soon have you jumping round
> Like a gazelle,' he says.
> 'Playing in the football team.'
> Quite undeterred by the sight of kilos
> Of plaster, chains, lifting-gear,
> A pair of lethally designed crutches,
> 'You'll be leap-frogging soon,' he says.
> 'Swimming ten lengths of the baths.'
>
> At these unlikely prophecies
> The old lady stares fearfully

At her sick, sick offspring
Thinking he has lost his reason –

Which, alas, seems to be the case.

Another visitor has still to call:

The sixth visitor says little,
Breathes reassurance,
Smiles securely.
Carries no black passport of grapes
And visa of chocolate. Has a clutch
Of clean washing.

Unobtrusively stows it
In the locker; searches out more.
Talks quietly to the Sister
Out of sight, out of earshot, of the patient.
Arrives punctually as a tide
Does not stay the whole hour.

Even when she has gone
The patient seems to sense her there:
An upholding
Presence.[6]

Many found in Josephine a reassuring and upholding presence. In their sickness and poverty, she proved dependable and did not fuss. In her encounters with others, I am reminded of the words given to me before my ordination by a priest with long pastoral experience of 'deep, difficult, holy work':

When you visit the Sick, or well Awakened, or dully Senseless, use no pre-contrived Knowledge or Rules, how you are to proceed with them, but go as in Obedience to God, as on his Errand, and say only what the Love of God and Man suggests to your Heart, without any anxiety about the success of it; that is God's work. Only see that the Love, the Tenderness, and Patience of God towards Sinners, be uppermost in all that you do to Man. Think not, that here Severity, and there Tenderness, is to be shewn; for nothing is to be shewn to Man, but his want of God; nothing can show this so powerfully, so convincingly, as Love. And as Love is the fulfilling of the whole Law, so Love is the fulfilling of all the Work of the Ministry.[7]

I have held on to these words and carry them with me as a reminder that the doing of Love's work calls for a particular kind of *attention* in relation to others, to see them mercifully, particularly the fragility of their existence and their quiet desperation in times of need. Plenty of things get in the way of seeing mercifully – not least an abiding preoccupation with ourselves.

Two little anecdotes: Noel Coward, meeting an old friend whom he had not seen for a long while, said, 'We have not got time to speak about the both of us, so let's talk about me.'

Then there is the tale of the disconsolate soul who wrote to a famous Rabbi, the Lubavitcher Rebbe, that he was deeply unhappy: 'I would like the Rebbe's help, I wake up each day sad and apprehensive. I can't concentrate. I find it hard to pray. I keep the commandments, but I find no spiritual satisfaction. I go to the synagogue but I feel alone. I begin to wonder what life is about. I need help.' The Rabbi sent the letter back, underlining the first word of each sentence. And it is always the same one, 'I'.[8]

The first requirement that enables us to see others as they truly are is to get ourselves off our hands in order to recognise their dignity and respond to their hurts. The next step is to exercise what we might call our moral imagination, so that we think and feel our way into the truth that we belong to each other and there are no strangers in a world where all are sisters and brothers of the Most High. Liberated by this truth, we begin to see the pathos that attends most lives.

Speaking on this theme a couple of weeks ago to a large group of Anglican preachers, I referred to the plight of Willy Loman, the central character in Arthur Miller's modern classic, *Death of a Salesman*. First staged in 1949, the play reveals Willy as an ageing salesman, no longer able to earn a living and struggling on a small commission. He has been obsessed by the American Dream of money and success but chose, unwisely, to go into the sales business. Despite the support of family and friends, he becomes depressed and delusional and makes attempts to kill himself that finally result in suicide. On the surface it is just one more death meriting no more than a by-line in the newspaper. But in the play, Miller demands that we look at Willy differently:

> I don't say he's a great man. Willy Loman never made a lot of money. His name was never in the paper. He's not the finest character that ever lived. But he's a human being, and a terrible thing is happening to him. So attention must be paid. He's not to be allowed to fall in his grave like an old dog. Attention, attention, must finally be paid to such a

person. You called him crazy ... But you don't have
to be very smart to know what his trouble is. The
man is exhausted ... A small man can be just as
exhausted as a great man.[9]

Attention, attention, attention – not a military order but
the plea of the playwright that we recognise that the great
dramas of existence – its achievements and joys, its tra-
gedies and unfulfilled hopes – parade before us in the
ordinary and everyday, often unrecognised. A long time
before Willy Loman, the world received another story
from the greatest teacher ever. The tale is too well known
to be told in full here and a testimony to its abiding power
is that even in an ostensibly secular age, many people still
understand what is meant by the term 'Good Samaritan'
(Luke 10:29–37). Its importance for me here lies not in
the compassion of the Samaritan who was moved with
pity, instead of walking by on the other side, but in the
arresting opening sentence of the parable. In response to
the question, 'And who is my neighbour?' Jesus replied:
'A man was going down from Jerusalem to Jericho and fell
into the hands of robbers, who stripped him, beat him,
and went away, leaving him half dead.'

The parable begins with the introduction of a man on a
journey. He is a central character in the unfolding drama
and in an isolated place suddenly becomes desperately
vulnerable. Significantly, Jesus does not tell his listeners
the name of the man. His identity is withheld and they
have to decide whether they feel sympathy for him or
identify with him. He is a traveller whose world is shaken,
a human being in distress, a man with no name, who
nevertheless has a claim to our attention because he is a
fellow sufferer, making his way like the rest of us through

a naughty world and coming to grief. The kindness of the Samaritan invites emulation – 'Go and do likewise' (Luke 10:37) – but the plight of the traveller and the response we make to his downfall, reveal the extent and depth of our moral imagination and our solidarity with all the nameless, broken individuals who, for whatever reason, fall by the wayside. Some of the people who come to me for help I know by name and, in the case of strangers, I make a point of asking. This is not about curiosity or security but the acknowledgement that we are travelling the same road, and sooner or later, we are exposed to calamities along the way.

A couple of years ago I spent some time in New Haven, USA, a fairly prosperous city on an upward curve and home to Yale University, one of the most prestigious 'Ivy League' centres of learning in America. In between business and teaching, I would occasionally sit in a coffee house across the way from the university and watch the minutes unfold on the busy street. There was plenty to see, with occasional moments of drama involving police officers, handcuffs and bodies being wrestled to the ground. My most vivid memory, however, is of the 'street people' of New Haven – the poor, aimless and homeless – making their way with monotonous regularity up and down the same block, pushing shopping trolleys with paltry items of food and clothing inside them. At scheduled times there was the queue for the church soup kitchen. In between there was only the park bench or the shuffling of feet as trolleys once again began their predictable journey of a few hundred yards before turning around to return to base. They would stop at the corner of the Yale campus, with its sweet smell of success underpinned by a financial endowment of 20 billion dollars.

Wealth and poverty stood conspicuously side by side with an immense chasm between them. The faces of the poor would be familiar to many passers-by working in the city but few, I suspect, would have any knowledge of the street people's lives or names. When I think of this scene I remember another image from the turbulent 1960s in America when black men denied equality would walk down streets bearing the placard 'I AM A MAN'. We are still a long way from realising that part of the American Dream vouchsafed to Dr Martin Luther King, Jr on 28 August 1963 when, in front of 250,000 people, he spoke so passionately of freedom, human brotherhood and an end to oppression. More than forty years on, we still find it easy to miss Willy Loman in the crowd and easier still to forget that he has a name.

For reflection

Today's poor children, unlike those of the Victorian era, are a minority, but they might as well be living on a different planet from their affluent contemporaries. One group is more protected, more fretted over, more lavishly provided for than any generation in history. Their parents pore over child-rearing manuals, go to astonishing lengths to secure places in the 'best schools', hire private tutors, fill every spare minute with improving activities, provide broadband connections (with internet access carefully supervised, naturally) and maintain constant vigilance against paedophiles and speeding motorists. One headteacher has called them 'helicopter parents', keeping their children's lives in general and their education under perpetual surveillance.

For the poor children – and I accept these are generalised caricatures to which there are many exceptions – contact with adults is confined to occasional shouting and slapping. They miss out on sports or drama clubs or learning musical instruments, fail to do their homework, turn to cigarettes and booze, and spend most evenings hanging out with their mates on the street. They are the sort who end up in trouble with the police and who suffer most of the ill-treatment – for example, the nose, rib and thumb holds used in young offenders' institutions – of which the UK children's commissioners complain in this month's submission to a UN committee (see 11million.org.uk under 'adult info').

Peter Wilby, 'Suffer the poor children'
in *New Statesman*, 16 June 2008

- How do we react to this passage?
- To what extent does it reflect or differ from our own understanding of the divide between rich and poor in Britain today?

To ponder

Read the parable of the Good Samaritan (Luke 10:29–37).

- In the light of the previous chapter, in what sense, if any, has our reading of the parable changed?
- Where might we expect to find the Willy Lomans of our own pressurised and uncertain times?
- What do we really think and feel about the people selling *The Big Issue* and how much sympathy do we give them?

I saw a great church standing in the greatest city in the world ... There passed me into its warm inside hundreds and hundreds of all sorts of people ... with all their difficulties, trials and sorrows ... I saw it full of people dropping in at all hours of the day and night ... and often tired bits of humanity swept in. And I said to them as they passed: 'Where are you going?' And they said only one thing, 'This is our home. This is where we are going to learn of the love of Jesus Christ. This is the altar of the Lord where our peace lies. This is St Martin's.'

Part of Revd Dick Sheppard's vision in 1914 that shaped St Martin's as the 'church of the ever-open door' in the 20th century

● What does this vision have to say to us today and how does it compare with the vision of our own church and congregation?

To pray

God of grace
give us wisdom and love to face hard choices with understanding and patience.
When our choice is wrong, forgive us;
when our choice is right, sustain us;
and when our choice brings us to disagreement,
keep us talking and listening.

Suffering Saviour,
who through the turmoil of despair and death opened the path to life for your people,

hear us as we pray for those bowed and burdened by
the harshness of circumstance,
that their despair may be ended and their hope made
anew.

Jesus, restorer of people,
who sought the woman out from the crowd that her
healing might be complete;
give us when we are oppressed by loneliness
a sense of our own worth,
a knowledge of your love,
and a word of friendship to lift our spirits.
Following your example, may we seek each other
out, and offer a word that heals.

From *Prayers for Mission, Hasten the Time*,
compiled and edited by Christopher C. Burkett
(USPG, 2001)

Chapter 4

⊹━━━⊰⊱━━━⊹

THE POLITICS OF
PARADISE

A N AFTERTHOUGHT AND A question came to me in
the light of the last chapter. What Josephine
impresses upon us through her dealings with others is the
duty of true *hospitality*, marked by an open response to the
dignity of every person. Confronted by the stranger and
the marginalised in the brief and unexpected encounters of
daily living, we are to receive them on their terms. The
world is a mysterious place but God's grace is everywhere
and is often to be found in the surprising, the disconcerting, the unwanted and the unlooked for. Our way
of looking at the world is frequently skewed by our
inability to pay attention to or accept what is new and
different. Reality amounts to rather more than our limited
vision and hospitality is about learning to read the world
better in order to discover our own place in it. Josephine
was able to do this because the still point of her life and its
purpose was grounded in silence and prayer. By waiting on
God, she came to see the beauty and value of every human
soul, especially the outcast and despised. Hospitality, she
reminds us, has less to do with conventions, rules or
feelings than the basic religious conviction that human

need of any kind is our business because 'God loves difference and, so at last, must we'.[1] To our considerable
surprise and perhaps even shame, the Willy Lomans on
our busy streets represent fractures in human solidarity
and testify to a broken society where the notion of the
common good as something we all share is easily eroded
and not everyone has an honoured place. The collective
state we are in depends on our ability to hold those who
are not like us within the radar of our moral concern.
Josephine, we remember, as a young girl, was shaped by
the teachings of the Hebrew Bible: in no fewer than 36
places it requires us to 'love the stranger' – partly because
we are to respond to each other's cries for help but also in
the humbling awareness that we encounter God in the face
of the unfamiliar.

Musing a little more on this notion of hospitality, we
are faced with the looming question of how we are to live
in this world. By 'world' I am not thinking only of global
market forces and the vagaries of economic trends that
dominate the news headlines. Globalisation with its gifts
and discontents is a new and extraordinary fact of our
time, but it is not the only fact. The larger world
addressed by this chapter acknowledges the place of
money, goods and power but also makes room for morality. It is therefore not indifferent to the interplay of joys
and sorrows that bind us to each other or the misfortune
and injustice that strike at hope and promise. Before
suggesting what this more comprehensive world requires
of us by way of response, I need to make a brief
digression.

Thinking about how we ought to live has been the
business of religion and philosophy for centuries. It is also
our business as persons in the making, perhaps even more

so in an age awash with the relentless soundbites, images and slogans that blight our imagination and understanding. None of us comes into the world with a moral compass and sooner or later most of us are confronted by questions of meaning – who and what we are, the mark we leave behind, the debts we owe to others and the sort of future we hope to make. Long-standing vegetarian that I am, with a sincere belief 'that everything that lives is holy', I am still clear that such considerations – making moral sense of our circumstances and choices – are decidedly human challenges that separate us from rats and rabbits or even the chimpanzees that share so much of our genetics. I know that left alone at the piano for an indefinite period of time, one of their number might knock out a passable tune, but I have no expectations that any chimpanzee, however cuddly or bright, could ever feel the obligation to rattle an Oxfam tin, sign an Amnesty International petition or march against weapons of mass destruction. The language of moral protest (like language in general) and the sentiments that move us to save the planet distinguish us from the animal order and remind us that for all our contradictions and capacities for damage, part of us longs to do the right thing and desires to be good. In this way we help to mend the world a little: we become, as Gandhi insisted we must become, 'the change we wish to see in the world', and from the stuff of our lives we may hope to fashion something that is decent and true.

For such ambitions to bear fruit, we have to work at the details, and it is here that Josephine offers us encouragement and guidance. Her faith, unlike that of some of her contemporaries who doled out charity whilst insulating themselves from the causes of poverty, is world affirming. She practises the religion of the Incarnation and immerses herself in the issues of her time. For the sake of the Word made flesh and the cause of the crucified One who relinquishes his kingship for the sake of the many, she becomes involved and engaged. Not in a superficial or uncritical way but 'energetically, wholeheartedly, salt-of-earthishly, often counter-culturally'.[2] Without ceasing to honour the story of the Good Samaritan, she moves beyond it.

She grasps that pastoral care and good works have their place but she goes further. She takes to heart the parable of the rich man and Lazarus (Luke 16: 19–31) with its jarring contrast between the man who is dressed in purple and dines sumptuously every day and the poor man who languishes at his gate covered with sores. It is not simply the absence of hospitality on the part of the rich man that moves her to act on behalf of those who continue to be neglected. It is the recognition that there are always people at the gate, and the prophetic task is to know whether they are the barbarians who crush the poor or Lazarus. Josephine finds evidence of both in the persistent disparity between great wealth and appalling squalor and the tolerance of the 'squalid activities of vice'[3] that allowed poor women to be traded like sheep to the slaughter in the slave markets of the great cities. In the name of justice she demands something better and dares to speak truth to power. She redeems her times with what she has to say and reminds us that the Christian gospel is diminished if we refuse to ask why the poor are deprived and what needs to be done in relation to the social and economic conditions that deny them the possibilities of justice.

In consequence, we misunderstand Josephine if we celebrate her as just one more ministering angel of Christ who was blessed with an abundance of virtue and compassion. She is remembered in the Church calendar on the day of her baptism, 30 May, as a *social reformer*. This was her greatest achievement. As a friend of the world she cherished its beauty and stood alongside the powerless. But she was stern in her condemnation of fundamentally unjust legislation that perpetuated poverty and prostitution, and she demanded change. She would have agreed with Augustine that without justice, governments of whatever persuasion, 'are gangsters on a large scale'.[4] It is only through the pursuit of justice – which for Josephine meant the struggle to render more fair, the economic, social and moral system in which we all live – that the vision of human flourishing may hope to be realised.

I think we need a picture at this point to grasp why in the end, for Josephine, everything came down to justice. In late 1874 she made a European tour to gather wider support for the repeal movement. She took in Paris, Rome, Naples, Florence, Milan, Turin, Geneva and Lausanne. An exhausting schedule necessitated endless meetings with politicians, clergy, doctors and the press. Not everyone received her gladly and she had to cope with the hardest European winter for many decades. The fog and cold chilled her heart and made the struggle seem even harder. The few hours at her disposal were spent in the cold polishing her French and Italian and learning her speeches by heart so that her arguments carried weight and were not open to ridicule. In her pocket she carried a prayer written by George commending her to God's safe-keeping. She read it each night and it strengthened her. Just a few miles from Florence, in the town hall of nearby Siena, there was also a magnificent fourteenth-century fresco by Ambrogio Lorenzitti to inspire her. Entitled the *Allegory of Good and Bad Government*, it depicts on the one hand a vision of the well-run state where citizens live in harmony because 'lady Justice has stripped the wicked of all power', and on the other a blighted landscape where a wolf-like figure, Fear, stalks the city because Justice is bowed and her scales broken. The profound sentiment expressed in the fresco is that peace, community and the good life flow from justice and not the other way round. An inscription in Latin on the fresco translates as 'Love Justice, you who judge the earth'. This was a text to warm Josephine's heart in the deep mid-winter, with the power to evoke days long ago at her father's side when he taught her the moral duty of creating a fair and decent world.

The pursuit of social justice is a tough call and one, frankly, that many of us would prefer to side-step and concentrate instead on good neighbourliness, kind deeds and practical service. This, after all, is what local churches do best: in quiet and often unremarkable ways they mend broken hearts and bind up the wounded. But if we leave it there and choose not to pay attention to trends or policies that blight human lives or make for more inequality, we should not pretend that we have honoured Josephine Butler or taken to heart the message of Jesus and the prophets that speaks of a new order where the poor will be blessed and the hungry filled. At the very least we should be ready to challenge those who govern us. Politics is too important to be left to politicians and we need to think in questions. The Chief Rabbi, Jonathan Sacks, provides us with a useful list:

> Of any economic system we must ask: Does it enhance human dignity? Does it create self respect? Does it encourage creativity? Does it allow everyone to participate in the material blessings of this created

world? Does it sustain a climate of equal regard – for employees as well as employers, the poor no less than the rich? Does it protect the vulnerable and help those in need to escape the trap of need? Does it ensure that no one lacks the means for a dignified existence? Do those who succeed share their blessings with those who have less? Does the economic system strengthen the bonds of human solidarity? And does it know its own limits – does it recognize that its values are not the only values, that there is more to life than a perpetual striving after wealth, that the market is not the only mechanism of distribution, and that an economic system is a means not an end?[5]

Ten questions that read like a social, spiritual and moral audit. If we close our eyes we can almost see Dr Sacks coming down from Mount Sinai like Moses of old, clutching them on tablets of stone as the means of our collective well-being! The angel in us immediately recognises their relevance and importance for human community, but the darker element in our nature evades the challenge. 'Such immense issues,' we murmur to ourselves, 'and so little by way of resources and organisation to master them.' It can feel too exhausting and what, we ask, can an individual or small group realistically hope to achieve when pitted against the corridors of power?

There are three things we can do. We can remember, firstly, the importance of the individual in the pursuit of an ideal. From pastoral initiatives that began as small-scale, local and particular, Josephine moved from the care of the homeless and sick to a public arena where eventually she enlisted the support of thousands and rid her nation of a hideous stain. The power of one inspired by a vision is no trifling thing. Even, or perhaps particularly, in a globalising world dominated by impersonal economic forces, Josephine encourages us to feel our strength and believe in our ability to shape the future: 'Do not imagine you are powerless ... do you believe it is possible that the just and merciful God will leave us helpless?'[6] Secondly, we can avoid the temptation to be preoccupied with organisation – the seductive and draining idea that until everything is in place, nothing can be done. Josephine had little time for endless talk or the recording of minutes that took hours and contributed little or nothing to the task in hand. Speaking to delegates at Exeter Hall where, as she reminded them, the task was nothing less than a revolution, she comments:

> While speaking of organisation, will you suffer me to sound a note of warning? In my own life's experience I have frequently seen that *life*, living power is sacrificed to the perfecting of organisation. You may perfect your organisation to the utmost; but if not filled and permeated with life, it will not bring about a single reform ... People are apt to become too busy and absorbed with it; and when they succeed in getting it into beautiful working order they contemplate it with satisfaction and are tempted to conclude that it must be doing a good work, while sometimes it is doing nothing vital ...[7]

What Josephine would have us avoid is an over-emphasis on machinery, and thereby beginning at the wrong end. It is easy with such an attitude to forget the essential thing – and this constitutes my third point – the power of the unseen Spirit that is capable of breathing life into the driest of bones to make them live. Rules, sound finances and good policies have their place but first we should seek passionate and energetic collaborators who recognise the urgency of the moment and the duty to act. Then, 'Our Father in heaven who knoweth that we have need of material resources ... will justify the faith that steps boldly forth, long before all these things are seen visibly to exist'.[8] The words read and sound like a summons. They breathe the pilgrim air of the Old and New Testaments and remind us that just as good things flow from justice, so it is that money and organisation follow vision. By equipping ourselves with 'the whole armour of God' (Eph. 6:11), we are more powerful than we dare imagine. Powerful enough, in fact, to defend lady Justice against tyranny, cruelty, indifference and deceit. Much has changed since Lorenzetti painted his majestic fresco six centuries ago, but it remains the case that a better life for the many depends on a vision where social justice and equality under the law remain the hallmarks of our local communities and wider civil society.

With regard to the earlier question concerning how we are to live in this world, my reading of Josephine has identified true hospitality and a love of justice as the offerings she makes to us as we stand with the unloved and powerless of our day. As social reformer and prophet, she can help to shape our lives and dignify our purposes as we look to the 'bright morning star' and the mandate to make 'all things new' (Rev. 22:16; 21:5). I also believe that her morally tough and unsentimental approach to matters of life, faith and self-centredness still has much to teach us.

Despite being born into a respected and affluent family, Josephine, for most of her years, lived a fairly frugal existence and rarely enjoyed the trappings of wealth. There was her husband's modest income but there were also three sons to be educated and social projects to be financed. In truth, a good deal of what they had they gave away. Josephine sold the few jewels of any worth that she possessed; the annual income she received from her marriage settlement went on the House of Rest in Liverpool; George earmarked an eighth of his annual salary for charitable and educational purposes; periods of convalescence following arduous and exhausting campaigns were paid for by friends, relatives or fellow workers.

Today, when the rich still have too much and the poor too little, Josephine would be making the case for living simply. In a culture where iPods, mobile phones, plasma TVs, computer games and home entertainment systems have come to be regarded as essential, she would encourage restraint on our part. Not because she is against pleasure – this, we need to remember, is the beautiful woman who captivated onlookers on the dance floor and entertained guests at the piano – but simply as a principled statement against excessive greed. My guess is that she would be behind Modest Living, a new moral movement launched by Bob Holman, Christian Socialist and community worker, who is calling on his fellow citizens to live according to 'need rather than greed'.[9] Of course, this sounds a bit utopian, quaint and naïve when consumerism has so powerfully shaped the argument concerning what it means to be human. On this view, our deepest need, apparently, is for regular retail therapy and our purpose is to shop. Even when the planes slammed into the twin towers on 9/11 2001, the best advice the President had for the people of New York was to go out and spend. It is possible, however, to take a different view and sense a

growing unease concerning the unequal direction of
society and the plight of those who are struggling to
survive. In its recent discussion document, *How to Live in
the 21st Century*, the influential political pressure group
Compass informs us that 'half the UK's population shares
just 6% of Britain's wealth, while the top 1% own a
quarter of it; 3 million children live in poverty ... while
the rich's privileges seal them off from the rest of
society'.[10]

Because we know that Josephine paid meticulous care
to her arguments and made sure of her facts before she
engaged in her struggles against Parliament and vested
interests, we can be sure that she would have devoured the
Compass report. Protest and moral indignation are never
enough for her. We should be prepared to pay attention to
the details, dig a little deeper to discover who is doing
what to whom, for good or ill in rapidly changing times,
and be ready to do some hard thinking. In the fight against
inequality she tells us that it is not enough to be sincere,
for we might be confused or prejudiced in our sincerity.
The requirement is that we should hold on to our brains so
that we are clear what the issues amount to and why, from
a moral perspective, they matter and need to be
addressed.

In acknowledging this widening gulf in society and the
financial markets that exclude many from their privileges,
what, more specifically, would hurt Josephine now and
where would she be directing our gaze? I can hear her
voice in the campaign currently being led by Clara Osagiede on behalf of women cleaners working in the London
Underground. They are fighting for a 'living wage',
something more than the derisory £6.10 an hour they earn
on the night shift that carries no benefits, no pension, and

no sick pay – not even if they are assaulted on the job and have to take time off. Many of the women are of African origin without indefinite leave to remain in Britain. Since April 2007 they have twice taken strike action to protest about unhygienic working conditions, poor employment benefits and a wage that keeps them in poverty in the nation's capital, where the cost of living is estimated by the Mayor's Office to require at least an hourly rate of £7.45 to survive.[11] Clara Osagiede works five nights a week and shares a two-bedroom flat with five others and sleeps on the floor. They live in fear of the bailiff coming and taking what little they have. They also know that in a harsh and competitive global labour market, employers can afford to be hard on those performing menial but essential tasks, particularly if they opt to join a union. They are, however, quite literally, out of sight of public concern, working through the night on the Underground, as the citizens of London sleep on. Josephine would, I think, be concerned to wake them gently but firmly from their slumbers in order to alert them to the injustice beneath their feet.[12]

Apart from urging employers to adopt socially responsible standards, she would be giving her best energies to the plight of the thousands of women ensnared and trafficked across international boundaries in a global sex industry generating huge financial rewards for the kidnappers, pimps and dealers who inveigle innocent victims into conditions of servitude, cruelty and violence. In our time, the sexual slavery that became the great cause of Josephine's life is once again impressing itself upon the world with an alarming sophistication aided by modern developments in technology, communication and transportation. Since the mid 1990s there has been a disturbing upsurge in human trafficking. Women and girls come from poorer countries and former communist states thinking only of the bright lights and better life of Western cities. Some expect to work in the commercial sex or entertainment industry before moving on to opportunities that they are told will offer self-development. None anticipate slavery or a journey where women describe 'being kicked, burned with cigarettes, having their heads slammed against doors, being hit with bats, threatened with knives, dragged by the hair and punched in the face'.[13] Once established in Britain, they are in the hands of callous owners and the casual self-centredness of clients who do not care. To be clear: we are talking here about victims. Not the independent sex worker who has freely chosen to make a living in this way, but the women and children bought for £15–£25 'per half hour session against their will, multiple times a day'.[14] Theirs is a 'hell on earth' sustained by a consumer culture that is adept at 'teaching people to imagine that they want, desire, need a certain product or service'[15] and an elaborate network of international procurers, drivers, groomers, financiers, fraudsters, fixers, state officials and brothel keepers. The story is an old one but the scale of activity, cruelty and financial gain in an industry thought to be worth $12 billion globally[16] is unprecedented.

Now pause … After a long sigh or sharp intake of breath, try to entertain the fact that this is happening in our advanced democracy where citizens are ostensibly free to go about their business without fear or coercion, free to work, love, rest and pray. And then consider – for this, without doubt, is Josephine's question for us – how is such horror possible or permissible? To frame the question differently: what is happening that such a free market in sex has become acceptable? It seems that we have almost sleep-walked our way into a culture where sex sells and permeates everything, through computers, telephone booths, mobile phones, porn channels and magazines and the pages of our national and local papers. Lap dancing, massage parlours, personal services and escorts no longer seem a big deal and the procurement of sex becomes 'for some men as little worthy of remark as going to the pub on a Friday after work for a wind down and the start of the week-end'.[17]

We inhabit a culture of complacency, succumbing to what Rowan Williams describes as a 'comfortable innocence'[18] in relation to the brutalised lives of the world's vulnerable women and children caught up in the evils of trafficking. Josephine would be quick to point to the way in which the State has allowed the sex industry to develop in Britain with little or no regard for the damage done to those who find themselves trapped against their wishes in its activities. I can hear her saying, 'There is without doubt State accountability and something to be done in our political house about the disorder in the cellar.'[19]

But action is also called for, she would argue, on the part of agencies other than the State – the third sector of the religious, voluntary and civic associations with a professed care and concern for the safety, dignity, freedom and personal well-being of endangered individuals. We are back to the business of hospitality and our duty towards others who are different. Beyond compassion, we are also faced with the challenge of how we respond to our highly sexualised culture and the trade in bodies that denies everything Christianity affirms about the supreme worth and value of each person as a child of God. Josephine campaigned for the abolition of the Contagious Diseases Act. She had done her homework and her crusade was the answer. From this I can only conclude that in relation to the sex trafficking that is established in our towns and cities today she has but one question for us: what are we going to do?

For reflection

Josephine Butler opened her own home and then raised finance to run places of hope and sanctuary for those caught in prostitution. Are there things we can do locally or nationally to enable women to live without fear of abuse, violence or entrapment? To what extent does the issue of sex trafficking claim our time or priorities? Are our eyes open for violence against women in our midst – at the bus stop, the corner shop, the person in the next pew at church?

To ponder

Has no one condemned you?

When they kept questioning him, he straightened up and said to them, 'Let anyone among you who is without sin be the first to throw a stone at her.' And once again he bent down and wrote on the ground.

When they heard it they went away, one by one, beginning with the elders; and Jesus was left alone with the woman standing before him. Jesus straightened up and said to her, 'Woman, where are they? Has no one condemned you?'

She said, 'No one, sir.'

And Jesus said, 'Neither do I condemn you. Go your way, and from now on do not sin again.'

John 8:7–11

A children's prayer for slaves

Dear God,
No one is owned except by you
who made us, loves us, owns us too.

And no one is made less than pure
by what the world makes them endure.

And no one is loved less by you
through what they have been forced to do.

For no one is no one to you,
whatever life has brought them to.

And when they're freed to run to you,
they'll know, no one's no one to you.
Amen.

Lucy Berry

Litany for open eyes

Lord, open the eyes of my heart to see beyond
the woman standing on the street selling sex …
that *I* may see the pain, the shame,
the brokenness in the life of that woman.
Open the eyes of my heart to see what *I* might do
to understand better what brought her to sell
the only thing left, which is herself.

Lord, open my eyes that I might see.

Open the eyes of the Church to see beyond the sin,
to become community to the abused, to the homeless,
to those entrapped through prostitution and drugs.
Open the eyes of those with power and resources,
to provide financial support to projects working with
these women, so that an alternative way of life might
be possible.

Lord, open my eyes that I might see.

Open the eyes of my heart, Lord, to see my own
prejudice
and the preconceived ideas that would limit my
actions.
Open the eyes of those in despair, without hope,
in prostitution,
to see light in their darkness.

Lord, open my eyes that I might see.

Open the eyes of the sexually exploited
and those living on the margins of our society,
to know Jesus as their Lord and Saviour.
Lord, open my eyes, my heart, my resources,
that, seeing, I might feel; and feeling, I might –
along with the company of all the saints
here present praying with me
and praying with us in the heavenly city –
be liberated to serve you and liberate others
from bondage and despair.

Val Jeal

To pray

To you, Lord, we bring our thankful hearts.
All people will come to your table of welcome.
All nations will be refreshed by your cleansing water.

As we are called to sit down and eat,
we recall that we are all invited as guests
with those who are not remembered,
those who have been enslaved,
those who have been sold and bought and beaten.

We call to you, as our host,
to bring all who are hungry for justice,
all who are crying for bread on their table
to be one with us at your great feast.

Carrie Pemberton

May the roots of faith grow strong within you.
May your vision of peace be like a clear sky.
May you be touched by the lightning flash of bright
hope.
May you drink deeply at the well of joy.
May the love of God
be your blanket and your pillow,
your bed and your room,
and may God's arms surround you
now and for evermore.
Amen.

Christina Rees

Further resources

You may be interested in the following further resources for resisting sex trafficking and the abuse of women and children in our communities:

www.notforsalesunday.org – for resources focused on this special Sunday, the third Sunday of each May. Further worship resources, downloadable media, ideas for youth groups and sponsorship opportunities can be found on this site.

www.notforsaleuk.org – to become part of the growing movement resisting sex trafficking and all its associated abuses. Not for Sale UK is a movement committed to seeing legislation similar to that enacted in Sweden, where clients of sexual services are prosecuted, rather than those being sold. Not for Sale UK is seeking individual and organisational partners from every sphere of society, every walk of life. In creating dynamic partnerships, Not for Sale UK seeks to create an irresistible force to enable legislation to prosecute those who demand sexual services for cash and undermine the freedom and dignity of every woman and female child by purchasing women for paid sex.

www.chaste.org.uk – the interdenominational charity Churches Alert to Sex Trafficking across Europe was established to create places of safety and recovery for those emerging from having been trafficked for sexual exploitation. CHASTE develops safe housing with partners across the denominations, provides counselling for survivors and leads training for those working directly with women who have been trafficked. Chaste is a founding member of the Not for Sale UK coalition, and leads Not for Sale Sunday. The webpages have a wide range of links to other church-based initiatives, NGOs and government organisations working in the field, and a rich range of research papers, events diaries and networking opportunities across Britain and Europe.

To support the work of Chaste you can give online at:
www.chaste.org.uk/donate

or send a gift to:
CHASTE Donate
2 Penn Farm Studios
Harshon Road
Haslingfield
Cambridge
CB23 I JZ

or make a phone donation at:
0845 456 9335

Chapter 5

THE TRUTH-SEEKING
HEART

I T WAS WITH SOME relief and pleasure that I finally
settled on the title for this chapter. I wish that I could
claim some originality in choosing it, but the fact is (and I
can hardly be less than honest given my concerns here!)
the idea came from a book that I have recently reviewed.
It seems to me that the truth-seeking heart is a precious
thing and represents a vital dimension of our moral and
social life. A society that forgets the importance of
truthfulness quickly falls apart. When lies and deceit carry
the day, relationships soon wither. Deception feels like a
personal assault – from whatever source – and trust, once
forfeited, is not easily regained. Trust is a consequence of
truthfulness and we should shudder at the prospect of
living in a world where either or both are abandoned.
Imagine a society where no word or gesture could ever be
relied on: 'questions asked, answers given, information
exchanged – all would be worthless'.[1] By lying we damage
ourselves as well as others and corrode our commitment
to the common good. Everything becomes doubtful when
telling the truth ceases to be important. We are unlikely to
go over the edge of a cliff on a rope, however vital the

purpose, if we cannot trust our partner to keep hold of the other end of it.

Our commitment to truth-seeking binds us together and enables us to stand. It forms part of what the poet Keats called our 'soul making' and represents our response to Christ who came into the world as a witness to the truth (John 18:37). St John, the ageing apostle who bears sublime witness to Jesus as the human face of God, reminds us that we are to love 'not in word or speech, but in truth and action' (1 John 3:18). To do less than this turns religion (and therefore life) into 'living a lie' and honours Satan, who Jesus called 'the father of the lie' (John 8:44).

Truth-seeking is tough work. It makes moral, spiritual, emotional and intellectual demands on our minds and hearts. In terms of discipleship, it means 'to work and speak and think' for the One who in word and deed became the unique agent of God's truth as he faced fears and lies in his final days on earth. Philosophically and morally it is best seen as that blessed impulse within the human spirit that needs to know what is actually the case in any given circumstances and refuses to settle for what it knows to be illusory or simply false. Politically, it is bound up with the costly and difficult task of 'unmasking the powers' – getting behind propaganda, lies and vested interests that diminish decency and play havoc with ordinary lives. Humanly speaking, I recognise it as the heart's desire to live authentically and deliberately so that when we come to the end of our lives we shall not discover to our surprise and dismay that we have not actually lived.

I first came across this idea of 'living deliberately' almost thirty years ago. It was coined by Henry David

Thoreau, a young American of arresting appearance[2] who in 1845 left the village of Concord, Massachusetts and lived in a small house built with his own hands by Walden Pond, just a mile away from the village and close to the woods. He was twenty-seven, disillusioned by modern life and manners and possessed by the need to confront 'only the essential facts of life'. He stayed there two years, practising self-sufficiency, recording the changing patterns of the seasons and writing prolifically on everything that took his eye. Nature, philosophy, religion, politics and economics all claimed his pen. He eventually became famous as the man who lived alone in the woods, pro-ducing a testament that remains a contemporary classic.[3] In his writings there is an extraordinary attention to detail. Nothing is inconsequential to him, whether it is the distant whistle of the railroad train, the cries of woodland crea-tures, the striped snake heading to the water, or the Spring thaw that makes the ice of Walden Pond 'crack and whoop'. By living deliberately and paying attention, he saw what many of us miss or even lack the ability to see. He was also concerned to save others from lives of 'quiet desperation', clouded by the rise of the machine, the coming Civil War and the growing antagonism between abolitionists and slaveholders concerning the rights of the Negro. Thoreau despised the hypocrisy of those who maintained a so-called 'peace' in their communities through petty, daily deeds of violence that harnessed slaves to their owners' ambitions. Living deliberately entailed for him, the duty of 'unmasking the powers', of perceiving the violence behind the established order, the enslaving nature of private property and the shams and delusions that masqueraded as 'soundest truths'. From his little cabin and through his daily walks and meticulously observed routines, he practised a gospel of self-sufficiency and argued for the value, power and dignity of the 'unfettered self'. Man was born free but everywhere he seemed to be in chains.

Thoreau died young at forty-four of consumption and met his death with a serenity admired by his contemporaries. Nature had convinced him that all things were bathed in a pure and bright light that transcended death. But there was also his personal testimony, his flag of conviction that waved defiantly to the end, alerting all those who would listen to the task of confronting 'reality' – a word that rings through his work:

> Let us settle ourselves, and work and wedge our feet downward through the mud and slush of opinion, and prejudice, and tradition, and delusion, and appearance ... till we come to a hard bottom and rocks in place, which we can call reality. Be it life or death, we crave only reality. If we are really dying, let us hear the rattle in our throats and feel cold in the extremities: if we are alive, let us go about our business.[4]

There is so much in this manifesto that Josephine would have endorsed. She never met Thoreau but as he walked in the woods of Walden, she was spending anguished hours in the woods close to her Northumberland home, troubled by issues of injustice and wracked by questions for which there were no easy answers. In the mid 1840s she was still young and confused but even in her late adolescence it is possible to detect a craving for reality. 'Half sick of shadows', she longed, like Thoreau, for authenticity and cared little for the trifles and baubles that dominated respectable lives. She grew to live deliberately, making full use of the hours and increasingly adamant that her life would not be fettered by prejudice or delusion. She kept her eyes fixed upon real situations with the aim of seeing the world as it is. More than anything, as her later crusade demonstrated so powerfully, she embraced the cause of truth.

She drew inspiration from the American 'abolitionists' and her own followers eventually adopted the same epithet for their work in England. Josephine repeatedly made the connection between Negro slavery and white sexual slavery. Delegates came from America to support her cause and she found strength and comfort in 'the labours and fortitude of the heroes of the great American con- flict'.[5] Time after time, her speeches reflected the American experience. The declaration of Abolitionist, William Lloyd Garrison became a personal mantra: 'I will be as harsh as truth and as uncompromising as justice. I am in earnest — I will not equivocate — and *I will be heard.*'[6] The 'mud and slush of opinion' and the deadening hand of tradition stood as giants to be slain. What mattered was truth before everything.[7] In her lifetime many likened Josephine to Joan of Arc, an English version of the Gallic saintly warrior. I prefer to think of her as a redoubtable example of Bunyan's Mr Valiant for Truth.[8] Not once, but many times, and frequently in the face of opposition, she made what Nadine Gordimer, writing from the context of apartheid in South Africa, has described as the 'essential gesture'.[9] She placed her finger, so to speak, on the cor- rupted part of the body politic and, in the name of truth, exposed what was shaming and cruel.

The nearest contemporary example of Josephine's truth-seeking heart has just died. The newspaper on my desk carries his photograph on its front cover under the heading, 'Speaking truth to power'. The picture is a side profile of an old man who has patently suffered. His beard is black and grey and his gaze suggests the pained wisdom of one who has seen beneath the skin of things. Alexander Solzhenitsyn did as much as any creative artist or writer could to topple the monstrous Soviet system that, under Stalin, destroyed millions of lives. His book *The Gulag Archipelago*, first published in 1973, exposed the atrocities of the labour camps and bore witness to the plight of forgotten prisoners unjustly incarcerated. Solzhenitsyn became the conscience of the Russian people. As a dissident he spent eight years in the camps, laying bricks and smelting metal, fighting for food and watching his fellow inmates being punished for the slightest impropriety. He came to hate the Marxist ideology that made such things possible and, armed only with his pen and an indomitable will, he exposed the 'arsenals of lies' that prevented his beloved Russia from breathing. In 1970 he was awarded the Nobel Peace Prize. His acceptance speech was entitled 'One Word of Truth'. The title was part of a Russian proverb, 'One word of truth outweighs the whole world'.

The comparisons with Josephine are instructive. Like her, he wrote copiously – in his case on a battered typewriter, always interleaved with carbon copies in case the secret police seized the manuscript. A good deal of his output was initially ignored, particularly by intellectuals and those in influential positions, who could not bring themselves to believe that Stalin was a pathological tyrant rather than a great wartime leader. Josephine's mission was similarly impeded by clever and powerful people or self-righteous prigs who could not or would not grasp that justice required a respect for the real. Under the surface of their respective campaigns, lay intense self-scrutiny, huge moral courage, an occasional tendency towards 'prickli-ness' and 'a sometimes unsettling disregard for the smaller and softer things in life'.[10] Neither thought they were better or wiser than other people and sometimes both stood and felt monumentally alone. They experienced many setbacks – we have already noted some of Josephi-ne's – but Solzhenitsyn faced the heat and cold of the camps, abdominal cancer and the fear that he would never have children or return from exile. He had three sons and in 1994 was welcomed back to the post-Soviet state. The moral here is not one of happy endings after tribulation but something more real and compelling. The task for the truth-seeking heart is to struggle and endure, not neces-sarily in the certainty of victory but in the knowledge that 'one word of truth' is to be preferred to the dishonest consolations of indifference, fantasy, self-pity and unwar-ranted despair that so often claim our allegiance.

The philosopher or sceptic will almost certainly want to lodge an objection at this point. It is one thing to admire those who sacrifice themselves for the truth, but it is still necessary to ask *how* they arrive at the truth when issues of great principle are at stake. Is truth more than the emo-tions or feeling? Where are its sources to be located and what part does the understanding play in the process? We can hardly forget that we are citizens of a post-9/11 world where many are rightly suspicious that claims to higher truths can easily mutate into obsession or religious fana-ticism. In scriptural terms, we are back to the famous quotation posed by Pilate to Jesus, to which he received no reply: 'What is truth?' (John 18:38).

It is clear from Josephine's writings that in her case, her understanding of truth emerges from an intense religious faith derived from a knowledge of God and an allegiance to the person and teachings of Christ. Introducing a collection of essays entitled *Women's Work and Culture* in 1869, she wrote:

> Once more I venture to say I appeal to Christ, and to Him alone, as the fountain-head of those essential and eternal truths which it is our duty and our wisdom to apply to all the changing circumstances of human society. Believing as I do that He is Very God, and that He was, in human form, the Exponent of the mind of God to the world, I hold that His authority must be higher than that of any man or society of men by whom the Truth which we receive – so far as we receive Truth from men at all – can only be transmitted. I believe all His acts to have had a supreme and everlasting significance.[11]

The introduction tells us something very important. The truth which guided Josephine owed little to churches, creeds or catechisms. It came 'direct from God'[12] and was therefore relational. It engaged her personality at the deepest level of existence, and in Christ she saw the love and compassion of God that she appropriated as an inward reality. Both sources of the divine spark animated her life, her thirst for social justice and her extraordinary compassion for the wretched and destitute. Her grandson and biographer, writing almost fifty years after her death, expressed this rather well:

> ... one might, with all reverence, put it like this. There was first a belief in God, amounting to an absolute knowledge of His existence; secondly, an equally firm conviction that Christ *was* God; and, thirdly, a very clear understanding of the Holy Spirit. Then, what was so impressive in her worship of the

first two Persons of the Trinity was their coalescence in her mind. For there will be noticed in some of the phrases of these later letters what can only be called an interchangeability of the Father and Son. And that was more wonderful because it was instinctive, not cultivated. She loved them both, not separately, nor equally, but as One. It is difficult to analyse further this tremendous endowment. There seems no need. It was so very simple. She *knew* God.[13]

The sceptic can again rush in here with an alternative interpretation of Josephine's experience. Perhaps she was deluded, the victim of a chemical imbalance in the brain or the projection of unconscious desires? Josephine would not be disturbed or affronted by such questions. She knew, with the philosopher and theologian Pascal, that 'the heart has its reasons that reason knows nothing of'[14] and that religious faith cannot be reduced to intellect alone in its pursuit of the truth. She grasped that truth did not emerge as the conclusion of sustained investigation or intellectual argument, but neither was it something that simply, so to speak, occurred to her. It was a passionate truth that, in the words of Psalm 100, had endured from 'generation to generation'. Aided by scripture and prayer, it represented for her a form of personal acquaintance that constituted a vital source and store of moral knowledge. The language of faith would describe this in terms of Christ claiming her for his own. It was now the truth *of* Jesus rather than the truth *about* him that captivated her. She was too clear-sighted, intelligent and questioning to boast that she had privileged knowledge of the mind of God, but she also knew that too much religious timidity or endless equivocation could never achieve great ends.

Another key insight emerges here. Faith without feelings is never likely to gain a real purchase on our lives or see truth as more than a tidy or unexceptional conclusion. It is worth remembering that to say 'I believe' is to commit ourselves unreservedly to whatever task the gospel places before us. The Latin *credo* has at its root the word *cor* (heart): believing and truth-seeking therefore amount to more than just words. They represent the movement of the 'heart towards God in the face of One who challenges us to a more genuine understanding of ourselves'[15] and the great disruptions of our times. We know that as Josephine immersed herself in complex issues, she was always conscious that in her conversations with God and lesser, finite minds, 'every faculty of the mind and emotion of the soul is called to its highest exercise'.[16] What is fascinating to me is that she managed to do this with all the attendant risks of being wrong, without succumbing to the single-mindedness that is often symptomatic of the second-rate or closed mind. She had a passionately cool heart. Her mind was open to fresh disclosures with a capacity for learning new things that were sometimes held to be shocking by more timid or conventional religious minds. Charles Darwin and his followers were not, for her, enemies of the Almighty; rather, 'they have helped us to a revelation of a wider universe, a larger purpose and a greater God than we had before realised'.[17] Her words and the tone in which they are expressed are still worth heeding today in the contemporary (and sometimes ferocious) debate concerning our human origins and ends. With regard to evolution and so much else, she dares us to become seekers and explorers. To do less is to refuse to live deliberately and to forfeit the promise of fullness of life to those prepared to worship God 'in spirit and in truth' (John 4:24).

For reflection

How would we respond to Pilate's question, 'What is truth?' and what resources would we draw on to shape our answer?

From our reading of this chapter, what are the chief characteristics of the truth-seeking heart? Or, to put the question another way, what, in particular, do we find most admirable in the lives of individuals such as Solzhenitsyn or Josephine Butler?

It is possible to imagine a society built on lies, where no promise was ever kept and no word could be trusted. What sort of steps are available to us as individuals to build up the trust that enables communities to flourish?

To ponder

I sit and look out upon all the sorrows of the world,
    and upon all oppression and shame:
I see the wife misused by her husband,
I see the treacherous seducer of young women,
I mark the ranklings of jealousy and unrequited love
    attempted to be hid.
I see these sights on the earth.
I see the workings of battle, pestilence, tyranny,
I see martyrs and prisoners,
I observe the slights and degradations cast by arro-
    gant persons upon labourers, the poor, and upon
    Negroes and the like:

All these – all the meanness and agony without end –
I sitting, look out upon,
See, hear and am silent.

>   Walt Whitman, 'I Sit and Look Out'

The night, the street, street-lamp, drugstore,
A meaningless dull light about.
You may live twenty-five years more
All will still be there. No way out.

You die. And all again
Will be repeated as before.
The cold rippling of a canal.
The night, the street, street-lamp, drugstore.

>   Alexander A. Blok, *Russian Poems*

A man said to the universe:
'Sir! I exist.'
'However,' replied the universe,
'That fact has not created in me
A sense of obligation.'

>   Stephen Crane, 'War is Kind'

My brothers, the love of God is a hard love. It
demands total self-surrender.

>   Albert Camus, *The Plague*

Go, my songs, to the lonely and the unsatisfied ...
Speak against unconscious oppression,
Speak against the tyranny of the unimaginative ...
Go to the hideously wedded,
Go to them whose failure is concealed ...
Go in a friendly manner,
Go with an open speech,
Be eager to find new evils and new good.

Be against all forms of oppression.
Go to those who are thickened with middle age,
To those who have lost their interest ...
Go out and defy opinion.

Ezra Pound, 'Commission'

To pray

O Lord God,
inspire, determine and enable
the intention of my life,
that it be to thine honour.

Seal it as the desire of my heart,
the purpose of my mind,
the goal of my whole strength
that it continue single, clear,
immutable.

O Lord, be this intention, THOU:
thy truth, thy work, thy love, thy glory.

Let it govern my words,
dwell in my thoughts,
purify my dealings,
occupy and redeem my time.

Let it bring Thee into all my ways
and the ways of those with whom I have to do,
Thyself, thy light, thy salvation,
thy wisdom, thy worship, thy blessing,
Today and always.

Eric Milner White, 'My God, My Glory'

Open Thou mine eyes and I shall see:
Incline my heart and I shall desire:
Order my steps and I shall walk
In the ways of Thy commandments.

O Lord God, be Thou to me a God
And beside Thee let there be none else,
No other, nought else with Thee.

Vouchsafe to me to worship Thee and serve Thee
According to Thy commandments,
In truth of spirit,
In reverence of body,
In blessing of lips,
In private and in public,
To overcome evil with good.

Lancelot Andrewes, *Preces Privatae*

Chapter 6

❦

OWNING UP

Q UITE POSSIBLY YOU FOUND the last chapter a little daunting. Exploring what truth is and why it matters is a taxing business, so congratulations if you've made it this far! By way of relief, I want to offer you a story at this point in order to engage your imagination and prompt some final reflections. It is taken from Dickens, one of my favourite authors, and concerns one of the characters from his novel *Bleak House*.

Mrs Jellyby (only Dickens could concoct such a name!) is a Londoner who has devoted herself to a great cause. Most of her working hours are geared to a project in Africa that she describes as the 'Borrioboola-Gha venture'. Her aim is to resettle impoverished Britons among African natives, all of whom will support themselves through growing coffee. She is adamant that no other endeavour is so valuable or worthwhile or would eradicate so many social problems in Africa and England at a stroke.

Dickens' purpose is not to draw our attention to a scatty project destined to fail but to Mrs Jellyby, a woman so immersed in her work that she has no time for her large family except Caddy, her eldest daughter. Caddy is conscripted as a secretary to the cause: spattered in ink, she spends endless hours answering letters and dispensing literature about Borrioboola-Gha. She grows to hate the word 'Africa' or anything that smacks of idealistic causes. In her bitter experience, 'cause' is just another word for the destruction of family life. Her father, Mr Jellyby, is a man not far from desperate measures – someone close to the edge of despair. He is surviving – just – but as the book closes, in our last glimpse of him he is resting his head despondently against a wall. We learn finally that the Borrioboola-Gha project has failed. The local king has sold volunteers into slavery in order to buy rum. The news does not dismay Mrs Jellyby, however. She finds a new cause to fill her days – 'a mission with more correspondence than the old one' – that will elevate her to the status of a permanent campaigner.

She is, of course, a gross caricature but with Dickens we must remember that along with all the other literary grotesques that emerge from his imagination, Mrs Jellyby is teaching us something vital about our human situation. Most of us probably know or have heard of individuals of either sex who bear a disturbing similarity to her. People who demonstrate serious concern for the world's woes but then become so fixated or obsessed that they lose friends and wreak havoc in the lives around them. The ones they love are driven in the opposite direction and, like poor long-suffering Caddy, grow to hate what is otherwise laudable. Historically, sons of the manse or vicarage have sometimes suffered in this way[1] and I can recall at least one student from my college days who found himself alone at the dining-hall table because his conversation invariably moved only in one direction and towards one issue.

We have to ask whether the Mrs Jellybys of this world, outwardly committed to works of compassion or reform,

are not at some deeper level driven by something dis-
quieting – a sense of personal inadequacy or failure or
even frustration with those around them, including their
families. A noble cause, especially when it seems con-
sonant with God's will or a higher purpose, conveniently
excuses or even justifies the neglect of others, however
close or personal. Wielding the weapon of truth is a
dangerous business and great care needs to be taken 'that
we don't kill more than falsehood with it'.[2]

I hope that you will not be surprised or offended if I ask
whether such a charge can be made against Josephine
Butler. The question is necessary because I value her life
and reputation and my aim throughout this book has been
to be honest concerning a woman who preferred 'truth
before everything'. In this spirit we have to recognise that
her loved ones did suffer because of her work. It cannot
always have been delightful to share the family home with
the lost, the sick and the dying, often at very short notice.
As a devoted husband, George in particular had to find
reservoirs of patience to enable Josephine to fulfil her
mission. Many times he missed her physical presence and
her conversation and frequently worried about her ability
to cope. There must have been private moments of anxiety
and frustration. The evidence we have, however, suggests
that he bore both with commendable Christian fortitude
and patience in keeping with his character that was widely
admired and respected. The same was not true, however,
of his eldest son George. In a letter dated 17 June 1905
there is evidence of bitterness and recrimination towards
his mother: her 'freedom to serve' had, in his view, been
secured by his father's unceasing toil, 'journeying to and
fro, ungrudgingly giving his time and help to smooth her
way, even to the fatal sea journey from Copenhagen when

he took the dangerous chill'.[3] He also resented how little time Josephine spent with him and his wife Mia following his father's death.

There is a difficult balance to be struck here. George Butler senior did pay a high price in relation to the great cause that so often took his beloved wife from his arms but, even as his eldest son conceded, he did so *ungrudgingly*. He was following the precepts of Christ and never imagined that discipleship was an easy matter of 'going to heaven on feather beds'. The resentment of George's eldest son must also be set in the context of the serious head injury he sustained in a riding accident in 1894 when he was thrown from his horse. He suffered a fractured skull and broken eardrum that subsequently led to a breakdown. For a number of years he 'was under a cloud, sad, depressed, sometimes warped and strange in judgement'.[4]

From Josephine's perspective, as she looked back on her life, her public work, strenuous as it had been, appeared 'quite secondary' to her bright family life, that had shared much joy along with tragedy. For myself, I am content to suspend judgement here. Certainly Josephine was proud of her role as wife and mother, and over the years she brought warmth, wit, beauty and wisdom to the family table. But in the knowledge of the burden of her campaigns and the enormous cost they exacted on her time, vitality and health, I do wonder whether her estimation of her public crusades as 'quite secondary' is perhaps a little wide of the mark and indicative of an understandable human desire at the end of her life to smooth a personal path that had often been hard and stony.

Josephine was not Mrs Jellyby. She did not lose her humanity or become a thing of horror to others. But the important lesson I take from the cost of her discipleship is the need to protect ourselves against an excessive zeal that, unchecked, can leave us resentful, dispirited and wholly lacking in love. When, like Josephine, we commit ourselves to the high work of the gospel, we need to do so with her necessary safeguards of prayer and silence but also with the awareness that the commands of Christ are strenuous. In living them out, they must always leave room for compassion towards ourselves and others. Good works and high ideals have the power to consume us. When they cease to be animated by love, they work against us. In my own ministry, I have had to turn ruefully and more than once to the wisdom of St Paul in order to remind myself that 'if I give away all my possessions or even give my body to be burnt but do not have love, I gain nothing' (1 Cor. 13:3). Josephine warns us that to follow Christ will sometimes feel unfair to the point of despondency. The world's needs, indifference and hostility will take their toll. Only by keeping our love at full strength and remembering that Christ also desires that his servants should seek refreshment and renewal (Matt. 11. 28) can we hope to sustain the long journey that bears the costly hallmarks of the kingdom.

Before we close this book on an intensely deep and driven life, there are two remaining issues to be addressed. I raise them because I want to be faithful to Josephine as a real person with strengths to inspire us and, no less, with limitations from which we can also learn. I want to ask first: was Josephine too much of a 'gifted loner' when it came to matters of truth, faith and worship? And secondly, if she was, in what sense did she lose out, particularly when her campaigns brought her to the point of exhaustion?

In her defence, there is plenty of evidence to show that Josephine was not sectarian in her thinking and was never slow to engage with groups or societies with whom she shared a common cause. She understood and valued the power of strategic partnerships and her organising skills drew on many talents and sympathies in Britain, Europe and America. She shared her hopes and fears with her beloved George and without his unwavering support she would have been diminished as an individual and less effective as a social reformer.

In relation to her Christianity, however, there is little doubt that her faith was largely a private and personal affair that served to separate her from other believers. John Wesley had pointed out a century earlier that there was no such thing as a solitary Christian, but Josephine refuted this claim by staying close to her experience of God and his revelation in Jesus. This, we remember, was her truth – the source of her 'truth before everything'. Consequently, the worship of the Church afforded her private opportunities for quietness and contemplation but not a great deal more. Its doctrines also made little impact on her life. Believing, for her, was an interior and personal activity without the need or duty to belong to a wider religious body or institutional framework. I sense a real loss here. In her search for truth and meaning she failed to recognise that a fuller understanding of truth always requires the fruits of others' labours. If we are serious about exploring the mystery of God in Christ, it is best done with others who, as the Church, aspire to be a community of truthfulness. The fundamental simplicity and conviction that Josephine brought to the love of God bypassed what the Church had to offer. Many still take this option today and we are witnessing a rootless individualism in the churches and beyond that favours private opinion and personal preference above the invitation to share in the accumulative wisdom and worship of a gathered congregation. By opting out, by choosing not to belong, it is then forgotten that truth is always in some sense an inherited affair. In a recent book, Rosemary Lain-Priestley comments:

> If we do not immerse ourselves in the regular retelling of the Christian story, how do we remember who we are and who God is? Without testing the boundaries of our belief against other people's thoughts and understanding, how do we know when we have grasped – or missed – the point? Is faith possible outside of this framework of checks and balances?[5]

In reply to this last question, it clearly is the case that many people retain a belief in God without crossing the threshold of the Church. Life is complex, busy and demanding and we can all think of the uncharitable and dark elements within religious institutions that keep people away. But once we have acknowledged the limitations and frustrating aspects of the Church, we must also concede that in its prayer and worship we are offered a deeper framework for our life and the treasures of a believing community. Lain-Priestley again:

> … I celebrate the Church's skill at holding in trust and retelling the stories of the Christian community, and encouraging people to find themselves in all of that. I recognize that the Church at its best does hold us, nurture us, teach us, feed us and provide us with an extended human family. I understand that it can

draw out of us what we believe, how we might live by it and how it might change us.[6]

Perhaps Josephine never saw the Church at its best – the formative experiences of her youth were not encouraging in this respect – and the finer points of theological discourse rarely detained her. But as she made her difficult journey, as she watched and prayed, often in turmoil, I cannot but think that her stance would have been strengthened by the recognition that truth is always two-eyed and truth-seeking is a communal task. Believers are better together. The goodness and truth of others is contagious 'and helps us to conform our lives more closely to the "Holiest of Holies", Jesus Christ our Lord'.[7] In sharing some of Josephine's disillusionment with organised religion, I have nevertheless come to know that congregations often house rather special people who carry on saying their prayers and doing love's work without fuss or the need for attention. We learn from them and are shaped by their example.

I have just received a letter from a priest enclosing a copy of his last sermon to his congregation, preached some years ago. It is an interesting and revealing address but I was intrigued and moved by his final memory. He writes:

> When I was in the Cathedral parish there was an old lady who suffered badly from arthritis and who moved with great difficulty and in considerable pain. In spite of everything she always managed to struggle to the 9 a.m. Mass each Sunday. On one occasion, I saw her making her thanksgiving afterwards and I went over to have a word. I said, 'I think you are marvellous the way you manage to get to Mass each Sunday, despite all your pain.' She smiled and then

pointed to the crucifix and said, 'He did all this for me. It's little enough I do for him.'

I have been ordained long enough to know that this is more than a sentimental story. I have met this elderly lady in others: the woman who would often be the only communicant at a Saturday morning service yet possessed of a devotion to the sacrament that made it a privilege to minister to her. The deeply traditional Anglican, suspicious of anything that smacked of needless innovation in worship yet inspiring me one evening as I saw her bent frame in the distance, pitted against a stormy night on her way to a Holy Week service. The congregation member in hospital, close to death who nevertheless found it quite natural to ask after my two sons and their well-being. And the parishioner, now largely confined to her home, who I know prays for me regularly and that in itself is a source of strength.

In her personal pilgrimage and the public campaigns she waged for others, Josephine dug deep into her own resources. Often she struggled; sometimes she received a form of assurance or strength that she knew came from a higher realm. But she needed, I think, to dig more widely in the rich soil of congregational life. There she would have found even more truth and unexpected treasures to enrich and sustain her in the company of God's friends.

For reflection

Assurance

My love, I hold you in imagination,
Either mine or yours

And it is stronger than remembered passion.
It uses memory with all its force.

O and the clocks go silent, time departs,
Now is forever here.
How delicate yet strong are our two hearts,
Mine beats for you now almost everywhere.

Only when my world is rent with storm,
Threatened by sadness or
Overcome by black words which can come
And threaten me with the inner, hideous war.

Only then, I've lost you, O but fast
A little flash of sun,
A hurrying memory returns you blessed
And our great love is stalwartly as one.

Elizabeth Jennings, *Timely Issues*
(Carcanet Press, 2001, p. 41)

- From our reading of these chapters, how would we describe the marriage of Josephine and George Butler?
- To what extent does the above poem reflect their love for each other and the partnership they forged together?

To ponder

Lo! God is here, let us adore
And own how dreadful is this place:
Let all within us feel his power
And silent bow before his face:

Who know his power, his grace who prove,
Serve him with fear, with reverence love.

Lo! God is here, him day and night
The united choirs of angels sing:
To him, enthroned above all height,
Heaven's hosts their noblest praises bring.
To him may all our thoughts arise,
In never ceasing sacrifice.

    Gerhardt Tersteegen, translated by John Wesley

- What do these words convey to us concerning the place of worship in the Christian life?
- What do we think Josephine lost by 'believing without belonging' to the Church?
- And finally: what have we taken from this portrait of Josephine that might help us to live more faithfully as followers of Christ?

To pray

O Lord, save thy people and bless thine heritage:
Govern them and lift them up for ever.
Day by day we magnify thee,
And we worship thy Name ever, world without end.
Vouchsafe, O Lord, to keep us this day without sin,
O Lord, have mercy upon us, have mercy upon us:
O Lord, let thy mercy lighten upon us,
As our trust is in thee.
O Lord, in thee have I trusted,
Let me never be confounded.

    Te Deum Laudamus

Notes

Introduction

1. *Beating the Traffic: Josephine Butler and Anglican Social Action on Prostitution Today*, ed. Alison Milbank (George Mann Publications, 2007).
2. Jane Jordan, *Josephine Butler* (John Murray, 2001).

1. Eminent Victorian: Ahead of Her Age

1. Psalm 42:2: 'My soul thirsts for God, for the living God. When shall I come and behold the face of God?'
2. J. Butler, *Recollections of George Butler* (London, Simpkin, Marshall, Hamilton and Kent; Bristol, J. W. Arrowsmith, 1892), pp. 56–7.
3. Ibid., p. 64.
4. J. Butler, *Woman's Work and Woman's Culture* (London, MacMillan, 1869), p. xxxi.
5. See Jane Jordan, *Josephine Butler* (John Murray, 2001), p. 104.
6. Ibid., p. 108.
7. Ibid., p. 118.
8. John Stuart Mill, 'The Subjection of Women' in *On Liberty and Other Writings*, ed. Stephan Collini (Cambridge University Press, 1989), pp. 199, 216.
9. Cited in Millicent G. Fawcett and E. M. Turner, *Josephine Butler: Her Work and Principles and Their Meaning for the Twentieth Century* (Portrayer Publishers, 1927), p. 82.
10. Ibid., p. 85.
11. Ibid., p. 105.
12. J. Butler, *Recollections*, p. 402.
13. *Daily News*, Wednesday, 2 January 1907.
14. Words attributed to Hensley Henson, Bishop of Durham, 1920–39.

2. Prayer, Passion and the Inner Life

1. E.g. the Oxford Movement (1833–45), led by John Henry Newman, which aimed at restoring the High Church ideals of the seventeenth century.

2. Teresa of Avila (1515–82), Spanish Carmelite nun and mystic.

3. Catherine of Siena (1347–80), Dominican tertiary, daughter of a Sienese dyer.

4. 1 Thessalonians 5:17.

5. Henry Scott Holland, Canon of St Paul's and Regius Professor of Divinity at Oxford (died 1918).

6. E. Moberly Bell, *Josephine Butler: Flame of Fire* (London, Constable, 1962), p. 178.

7. Galatians 6:2.

8. Psalm 9:18.

9. J. Williamson, *Josephine Butler: The Forgotten Saint* (The Faith Press, 1977), p. 96.

10. Millicent G. Fawcett and E. M. Turner, *Josephine Butler: Her Work and Principles and their Meaning for the Twentieth Century* (Portrayer Publishers, 1927), p. 29.

11. Jane Jordan, *Josephine Butler* (John Murray, 2001), p. 19.

12. Cited in Zadie Smith, 'Middlemarch', article in *Guardian Review*, Saturday, 24 May 2008.

13. St Benedict (480–550), patriarch of Western monasticism.

14. Pope Clement V (Pope from 1305), who made the controversial decision to relocate his residence from Rome to Avignon in France in 1309.

15. Josephine Butler, *Catherine of Siena: A Biography* (London, Dyer Brothers, 1892), p. 10.

16. See *Butler's Lives of the Saints*, ed. Michael Walsh (Burns & Oates, 1988), p. 126.

17. Ibid., p. 126.

18. Timothy Radcliffe, *I Call You Friends* (London, Continuum, 2001), p. 122.

19. Ibid., p. 122.

20. Butler, *Catherine of Siena*, p. 39.

21. Rod Garner, *Facing The City: Urban Mission in the 21st Century* (Epworth, 2004).

22. Robert L. Short, *The Parables of Peanuts* (HarperSanFrancisco, 2002), p. xi.

23. Garner, *Facing The City*, p. 103.

24. Aelred Squire, *Asking the Fathers* (SPCK, 1973), p. 143.

25. A. S. G. Butler, *Portrait of Josephine Butler* (London, Faber & Faber, 1954), p. 177.

3. Remembering the Poor: The Pastoral Task

1. See 'Suffer the poor children', *New Statesman*, 16 June 2008, p. 17.

2. Nicholas Holtam, *A Room with a View: Ministry with the World at your Door* (SPCK, 2008), p. 22.

3. Ibid., p. 22.

4. Ibid., pp. 22–3.

5. Jane Jordan, *Josephine Butler* (John Murray, 2001), p. 68.

6. Charles Causley, 'Ten Types of Hospital Visitor', in D. J. Enright, *The Oxford Book of Verse 1945–1980* (Oxford University Press, 1995), pp. 81–5.

7. Attributed to William Law (1686–1761), often referred to as the greatest post-Reformation English mystic. His best-known work, *A Serious Call to a Devout and Holy Life*, deeply influenced the Evangelical Revival in England. His followers included John and Charles Wesley.

8. Jonathan Sacks, *Celebrating Life: Finding Happiness in Unexpected Places* (London, 2000), p. 47.

9. Arthur Miller, *Death of a Salesman* (New York, Viking Compass Edition, 1958), p. 56.

4. The Politics of Paradise

1. Jonathan Sacks, *The Dignity of Difference: How to Avoid the Clash of Civilizations* (Continuum, 2001), p. 23.

2. Nicholas Lash, *Theology for Pilgrims* (Darton, Longman & Todd, 2008), p. 33.

3. Ladies' National Association Circular, 17 August 1885, from the office of the Federation, Neuchatel, Switzerland, quoted in Jane Jordan and Ingrid Sharp, eds., *Josephine Butler and the Prostitution Campaigns: Diseases of the Body Politic* (Routledge, 2003), iv., pp. 274–6.

4. Augustine, *City of God*, Book 4, p. 139.

5. J. Sacks, *The Dignity of Difference*, p. 89.

6. Jordan and Sharp, eds., *Josephine Butler and the Prostitution Campaigns*, p. 87.

7. Millicent G. Fawcett and E. M. Turner, *Josephine Butler: Her Work and Principles and their Meaning for the Twentieth Century* (Portrayer Publishers, 1927), p. 122.

8. Ibid., p. 122.

9. See the article by Melissa Benn, 'The Shift to Thrift' in *The Guardian*, Wednesday, 2 July 2008.

10. Ibid.

11. See 'The Fight for a Living Wage' in *New Statesman*, 11 August 2008, pp. 12–13.

12. Some steps are being taken to introduce the living wage across the London Transport network, but several companies running the Jubilee, Northern and Piccadilly lines have yet to comply.

13. Cited in a report published by the London School of Hygiene and Tropical Medicine. See the article 'Trafficked' in *New Internationalist*, September 2007, p. 5.

14. See Carrie Pemberton, 'Josephine Butler and the trafficking of Women Today' in *Beating the Traffic: Josephine Butler and Anglican Social Action on Prostitution Today*, ed. Alison Milbank (George Mann Publications, 2007), p. 169.

15. 'Trafficked', *New Internationalist*, op. cit., p. 6.

16. Ibid., p. 5.

17. Pemberton in *Beating the Traffic*, op. cit., p. 169.

18. Cited in Foreword of *The Real Scandal of Sex Trafficking: A Resource for Worship, Education and Action*, eds. Lucy Berry & Carrie Pemberton (Kevin Mayhew, 2008), p. 5.

19. Pemberton in *Beating the Traffic*, p. 170.

5. The Truth-Seeking Heart

1. Sissela Bok, *Lying: Moral Choice in Public and Private Life* (Vintage Books, 2nd edn, 1999), p. 18.

2. A resident of Concord described him as 'a young man with much of wild original nature still remaining in him ... He is ugly as sin, long-nosed, queer mouthed and with an uncouth, and somewhat rustic, although courteous manners. He seems inclined to lead an Indian life among civilized men.' Cited by John Updike in *Due*

Considerations, Essays and Criticism (Hamish Hamilton, 2007), p. 133.

3. Henry David Thoreau.

4. Updike, Due Considerations, op. cit., p. 141.

5. J. Butler, Recollections of George Butler (London, Simpkin, Marshall, Hamilton and Kent; Bristol, J. W. Arrowsmith, 1892), p. 227.

6. Jane Jordan, Josephine Butler (John Murray, 2001), p. 116.

7. Truth before Everything was the title of a personal pamphlet that she published in July 1897. It ran to 9000 copies and its 24 pages constituted both a call to arms and a restatement of her guiding principles.

8. One of the central characters in John Bunyan's famous allegory of the Christian life, The Pilgrims Progress (first published in 1678 with a final part added in 1679).

9. Cited by Fergal Keane in his autobiography, All of These People (Harper, 2005), p. 25.

10. Obituary in The Economist, 9–15 August 2008, p. 82.

11. Cited by A. S. G. Butler, Portrait of Josephine Butler (Faber & Faber, 1954), p. 47.

12. Ibid., p. 46.

13. Ibid., p. 174.

14. Blaise Pascal, Pensees, iv. 277. Cited in The Oxford Dictionary of Quotations (Oxford University Press, 1979), p. 369.

15. Rod Garner, Facing the City: Urban Mission in the 21st Century (Epworth Press, 2004), p. 143.

16. Jordan, Josephine Butler, p. 43.

17. Ibid., p. 40.

6. Owning Up

1. See, e.g., Edmund Gosse, Father and Son (Penguin Classics, 1986).

2. See The Hidden Ground of Love: The Letters of Thomas Merton on Religious Experience and Social Concerns (New York, Farrar Strauss & Giroux), p. 264. Cited on http:11 in communion.org/articles/ previous-issues/issue -40/mrsjellyby - and - the - domination of causes by Jim Forest.

3. Jane Jordan, Josephine Butler (John Murray, 2001), p. 294.

4. Ibid., p. 294.

5. Rosemary Lain-Priestley, *The Courage to Connect: Becoming all we can be* (SPCK, 2007), p. 74.
6. Ibid., p. 77.
7. Rod Garner, *Crowded Canvas: Faith in the Making* (Inspire, 2008), p. 136.